M000195054

"Refill is a blessed gift to the b̲ [...]
ings, prayers, and suggested actions don't take long but slow you down and lift
you up. Kirk Byron Jones is a gift to the church and the world."

> **—Margaret Marcuson**, author of *Leaders Who Last: Sustaining
> Yourself and Your Ministry* and *Money and Your Ministry*

"Refill is for all who hunger for God and spiritual renewal each day as we minister with others. The spiritual practices shared here are relevant for where we
live and serve. This is a gift to share with those who joyfully nurture your faith."

> **—Robert Pazmino,** Valeria Stone Professor of Christian
> Education, Andover Newton Theological School

"These short and pointed reflections offer wisdom and deep poetic vision, laced
with pure joy. *Refill* offers hope and courage for living and leading during this
precarious yet holy time."

> **—Sharon G. Thornton,** author of *Broken Yet Beloved:
> A Pastoral Theology of the Cross*

"Any leader who works with communities—educational, religious, office, or
family—should receive the gift of *Refill.* The themes and reflections are set
together like jewels in a ring and provide a coherent approach for daily enrich-
ment and renewal."

> **—Sarah B. Drummond,** Dean of the Faculty and Vice President
> for Academic Affairs, Andover Newton Theological School

"Morning devotional time with *Refill* fuels me for the daily spiritual rigors of
following Jesus. It is a 'blue ribbon' resource—I plan to gift every one of my
closest ministry colleagues with a copy."

> **—Sue Nilson Kibbey,** Director of Missional Church Initiatives,
> West Ohio Conference, United Methodist Church

"If you want to serve freely, lightly, and faithfully, these hope-filled and joy-
infused meditations are just what you need—and perhaps just what you didn't
even know you were looking for. Rejoice and be glad!"

> **—Patricia Farris,** Senior Minister, First United Methodist Church,
> Santa Monica, CA

Other Abingdon Press Books by Kirk Byron Jones

Fulfilled: Living and Leading with Unusual Wisdom, Peace, and Joy
The Jazz of Preaching: How to Preach with Great Freedom and Joy

{REFILL}

Meditations for Leading
with Wisdom, Peace, and Joy

Kirk Byron Jones

Abingdon Press

Nashville

REFILL:
MEDITATIONS FOR LEADING WITH WISDOM, PEACE, AND JOY

Copyright © 2014 by Abingdon Press

This book is printed on acid-free paper.

Library of Congress Cataloging-in-Publication Data has been requested.

ISBN 978-1-4267-9656-2

14 15 16 17 18 19 20 21 22 23—10 9 8 7 6 5 4 3 2 1

MANUFACTURED IN THE UNITED STATES OF AMERICA

For my grandchildren, Dinali, Nayeli, and Jackson.
Our choosing to be refilled, over and over again,
has a direct impact on the world we give to you.
I hope our renewal leads to you being proud and grateful.

CONTENTS

ACKNOWLEDGMENTS

Refill is a product of my having been renewed by the words and actions of countless persons. To them all I bow and offer thanks from under the bottom of my heart.

To have a publishing company move beyond accepting and respecting your offering to cherishing it is a wonderful gift. I have the sense of Abingdon Press having done just that with *Refill.* For this, I am deeply grateful to everyone at Abingdon who had anything whatsoever to do with *Refill's* release into the world.

I am especially thankful to Laura Wheeler, Kelsey Spinnato, and Jeff Moore. Your direct editing and designing expertise has produced what I believe is a wonderful book presentation, apart from the words rendered. My "lead cherisher" at Abingdon is Acquisitions and Development editor, Constance E. Stella. Connie took my collection and categorized them into groupings of three. It was a slow tedious chore that she had the audacity to call "fun!" All writers need to have such a soul playing on their behalf at least once in their writing career.

Introduction

I am grateful for this sequel to my book, *Fulfilled: Living and Leading with Unusual Wisdom, Peace, and Joy*. When that book was completed, I looked around and there were two large notebooks of material that had been used only sparingly. My sense was that ideas and questions that were important enough to preserve would never be presented. I determined that I would keep the notebooks and continue adding to them for my own challenge and growth. And, lo and behold, God has granted another chance to share with others, to dialogue with you.

I offer these reflections as someone who believes more deeply each day that by gracious divine decree, we are cocreators with God of our lives, vocations, and organizations. Such sacred cocreativity is continually enhanced by our choosing to become more deliberate and delighted with the cocreative process. We always have the option to ask different questions, live new applications, and feel less burdened and more joyful about it all. No matter what the particular personal, organizational, and cultural circumstances and demands may be, our living and serving are always as meaningful and satisfying as God inspires and as we choose.

I hope that your choice to read this book leads to more courageous choices integral to adventurous personal and social exploration, discovery, and achievement, including the choice to question cherished ideas, the choice to try something different, and the choice to aspire to be a better version of yourself each day.

My prayer is that you refill each day not with the same things, but new things, and that you do so, not because you have to, but because you want to and because there is no other way to dance with a God who moves lightly yet confidently in mysterious ways and who always and forever has new wonders to perform.

{ How to Use This Book }

Use this book as you would a *box of matches*. Let reflections strike new questions and ideas of your own that will cause you to level up and inspire you to extend the end of your presently perceived farthest range.

Use this book as you would a *sketch pad*. May the white spaces and margin of the text eventually be filled with lines and doodles of ideas and questions that are a thousand times more profound and provocative than the words already on the pages. In fact, I hope your reflections will be so rich and expansive that you will need another completely blank journal in which to dream and imagine.

Use this book as you would an *enchanted mirror*. As you listen to the musical selections suggested and those you select on your own, allow your mind to patiently gaze, inward and outward. Determine to see with soft and generous eyes whatever it is that shows itself to you to be seen. Be open to the ways these new sightings dig new depths within you.

Use this book as you would a *song book* that not only contains music you may find worth playing and singing but also has a section in which you may compose your own music, music perhaps containing notes you have never heard until now.

Use this book as a *playbook*. To the affirmations, exercises, and practices you read, add your own. Purposefully design and execute new behaviors that will grow you, your team, your church, or your organization, and in so doing, cause God Almighty to cheer!

Use this book as a *devotional*. There are prayers here, but they await fellowship with your prayers—and yearning.

CONTENTMENT

Start with Gratitude and Grace

It is true in many places and spaces of life: Nothing beats a good start. When I am preparing sermons, I am always extra careful with introductions. I know that I have just a few seconds to be gifted with the attention of listeners. The early moments of a message significantly determine whether or not people will pay attention and how. Similarly, a good start is important when it comes to track and field, especially sprints. A race can be won or loss in the first strides. Nowhere is a good start more important than at the beginning of your day. A word of advice: Start with gratitude and grace, and go from there.

Prayer

God, I choose to be grateful for a moment in time I did not earn, win, and may not even deserve. And, I choose to live it in the spirit of the grand grace in which it has been given. Amen.

See Aspiration and Contentment Dancing

The best rest includes a feeling of contentment: a sense of peaceful satisfaction about what we already accomplished, including the lessons we've learned from our mistakes and so-called failures. Some persons resist allowing themselves to feel content for fear of becoming complacent. Remember this distinction; contentment receives new dreams and visions, complacency rejects new dreams and visions. Contentment replenishes our energy and enthusiasm for the challenging new adventures up ahead. Contentment compliments aspiration.

See aspiration and contentment dancing together.

Freed from negative associations with complacency, we can more easily grasp the connection between aspiration and contentment. Letting ourselves feel satisfied is a critical key to letting ourselves and those we lead soar even higher. Unrelenting aspiration leads to exhaustion. Aspiration soaked regularly in the satisfying waters of soul contentment leads to continuing explorations and discoveries.

Affirmation

I gently and joyfully allow myself and others to aspire from a place of contentment.

Dig Deeper

Daily, we are duped into believing that greater wealth is a matter of acquiring more. Yet, the truth is that wealth is less a matter of what we have and more a matter of what we appreciate. Deepening appreciation entails our digging deeper right where we are. Digging deeper may mean becoming more devoted in a marriage, cultivating an established friendship, or choosing to hoist new interest onto an old job, thus refreshing and refashioning it in a way that transforms it and you.

It may be that you are standing on what you are searching for. Dig deeper!

Practice

Think of three ways you can enrich a long-held but underdeveloped relationship, vocational focus, or general interest.

3

{ AWARENESS }

Listen for Everyday Glory

Once as I stood in a post office completing a form, another customer walked in. I couldn't help but overhear the conversation between the woman who had walked in and the postal agent. They knew each other. Besides exchanging the regular pleasantries, the postal agent asked about the woman's mother. The woman said that her mother was well. She went on to say that her mother was outside in the car and would probably come in were it not for errands that needed to be completed. "Tell her I said hello," said the agent. "I will," said the woman, and she walked out. A few moments passed, and I finished my writing. I turned to walk to the service counter and suddenly another person walked in. She smiled. When the agent saw her, she came from behind the counter and the two women hugged each other. The mother had time, after all, to greet an old friend and to smile at a stranger.

When the agent returned to her post, she told me that she'd known the woman for many years; she used to deliver her mail. The agent said, "She was always so nice; always cooking and asking me to come in and have a bite." I easily imagined them seated at a table, chatting and snacking together. What does this simple meeting in a post office have to do with anything? It illustrates that there is always a whole lot of glory going on, if we are willing to listen.

Practice

Focus on listening at a wider range this week.

Rushing Is Overrated

Watching the snow fall that morning in March, I was enthralled by the diversity of the size of the flakes, the quantity of their clumps, and the changing pace at which the snow fell. It was a wonderful display, unscheduled and free, just outside my window. Like anybody, I had planned things to do that morning, but watching the snow was not one of them. Yet, after it was all said and done for the day, that soft, scintillating moment of simply waiting and watching was one of the highlights of the day.

There is wonder to be had in waiting. Rushing is overrated.

Affirmation

I will embrace the grace of living at a sacred pace.

God Is Everywhere

If you're just spotting God in the "sacred" or "religious," you're not looking hard or soft enough. God is as much in the mud as God is in the rainbow.

Prayer

Dear God, I have been taught to believe that you are in certain places all the time and absent from certain places most of the time. Help me remove this ruse from my life, that I may be on alert for you whenever, wherever. Amen.

{ STILLNESS }

No Sitting; No Soaring

I'd been in the hotel room only a few minutes when I noticed two paintings of birds on the wall. I could tell from just glancing at them that they were probably painted by the same person; I was right. The paintings had a lot in common: The birds were portrayed in great detail, many colors were used, and most interesting of all to me, in both pictures the birds were perched on tree limbs.

As I stared at the images, a question popped into my head: In the artist's mind, have the birds just landed or are they readying themselves to fly? After more careful examination, I concluded that I couldn't be certain one way or the other. As I began to turn away from the paintings, I discovered that though I was done with them, the paintings were not done with me. Suddenly, the following thought landed in my mind: Whether having flown or preparing to fly, if the birds in the picture flew without ceasing eventually they would fall to the earth in fatal exhaustion. No sitting, no soaring.

Just like the birds, our soaring is dependent upon our sitting. Activism and achievement are dependent upon respite and contentment.

Action

Identify your favorite ways of being at ease.
Practice them more.

First Home

Sometimes
in stillness
you end up
in a place
that feels
more like home
than home.

Practice

Take a moment to be free of all burdens.
As you begin to relax, fall into the feeling of
being completely at ease. The sense of pure
peace may feel like a homecoming. We derive
from God's Center of Peace and Power.

Swamp Stuff

My native Louisiana is filled with swamps called bayous. Some of these swamps are rich in soil, foliage, and wildlife. Others are not so rich. The soil is contaminated and the life is snuffed out by rot and stagnation. So there are good swamps and bad swamps. If we are not careful we can become people of the swamp of the latter variety. I have in mind our allowing ourselves to be filled longer than we need to be with the mental sludge of messy memories, grimy grudges, dirty doubts, and filthy fears—swamp stuff. When we don't empty ourselves daily of such things, we become walking swamp people, living with things inside of us that can make us sick.

Swamp stuff can steal your song and take your dance. Swamp stuff is energy sapping.

Swamp stuff is a threat to enthusiasm and vitality. Swamp stuff will drag you down and stunt your every effort to get back up.

So, beware of the swamp stuff. Step into the Spirit instead.

Action

Practice emptying. Find a quiet place to focus on slowing and stopping your thoughts. As thoughts enter your mind, even positive ones, hush them. Your objective is to experience an extended moment of complete mental cleansing and peacefulness. The refreshing will both surprise and inspire you.

IDENTITY

Own Your Voice

I was on that path of imitation, wanting to sound exactly like Betty Carter. Wanting to be that. Nothing was more important than Charlie Parker. And he [Steve Coleman] said to me, "Well, that's true: Charlie Parker is very important. But who are you?" And that was the beginning, really, for me . . . the beginning of thinking about what my contribution was going to be. What's my expression going to be like?

—Cassandra Wilson, jazz singer

Action

Listen to a selection by Cassandra Wilson. Identify primary features of her voice. After you have listened and analyzed her voice, contemplate the uniqueness of your leadership voice and style. How can you own who you are most deeply, more deeply?

10

Standing with Harp and Sword

I have been in sorrow's kitchen and licked out all the pots. Then I have stood on the peaky mountain wrapped in rainbows, with a harp and a sword in my hands.

—Zora Neale Hurston

Action

Journal a response to Zora Neale Hurston's words.
What do you hear her saying?
What are the truths behind the images she paints?
What are your harp and sword?

Play Your Song

Art Tatum was a self-taught pianist whose recording career lasted from the 1930s through the 1950s. He is generally acknowledged to be one of the greatest two or three jazz pianists ever. Tatum's style was characterized by stellar technique and tenaciously creative chord combinations. To hear this partially blind dynamo of a musician is to be duped into believing that there are two persons playing, not one.

Tatum's greatness did not block him from appreciating the greatness of others. He once told Oscar Peterson (another jazz pianist on most short lists of great players), "Listen, there's an old man in Kansas City. He knows only one chorus of the blues. The man can't play the second chorus. And every time I'm there I go to hear him because nobody plays the blues like him. Everyone has something to say in music—if he has some talent and has the discipline to master even one chorus."

"Everyone has something to say in music." Another way to say it is, "Everyone has his or her song." No two songs are alike. If you don't play your song, the world loses the opportunity of ever hearing that song. So play it. Be who you are and who you are becoming in grand tone and style.

Action

Take a moment to reflect on your life as a song. What genre(s) of music would it be classified under? Give a title to your song. If you are satisfied with the music, think of ways you can play it with greater confidence and passion. If your song troubles you, begin to hear and play a new song.

{ PLAY }

Feeling Fresh Energy

When he was much younger, our son, Jared, used to greet each morning with the declaration, "I waked up!" He was genuinely excited about having another chance to be alive and have fun.

Anticipation and excitement need not be limited to childhood, sporting events, and holiday seasons. It is possible to deliberately create significant levels of anticipation, excitement, and fulfillment on a regular basis by remembering to focus on three simple but strikingly powerful life-enhancing practices:

1. Be Grateful. Life is something we never see coming and never know when is departing. By being grateful on purpose we acknowledge the gift of life and reenergize ourselves at the same time.

2. Look to Explore. There is no finding or creating passion and purpose in life without exploring. Each day offers the chance to discover and engage something new, even if we are in the same place doing the same thing. New adventures and discoveries have more to do with inner attitude than outer location.

3. Own Your Joy. As children we never hesitate to express our full feelings about being fully satisfied. Being free to express our joy enhances our experience of joy.

An Alternative to Pushing, Straining, and Striving

There is no living and leading without some pushing, straining, and striving. Childbirth usually entails its share of each. But to live life in chronic strain is to put undue pressure on ourselves and those who live and work around us. To counter the stress of feeling constantly under pressure, we simply need to reclaim something that is within us from the beginning: a spirit of playfulness.

As you recover your innate playfulness, resist thinking that your life will lose the edge and advantage we believe constant pushing produces. Living with a playful spirit cultivates lightness of heart, touch, thought, and speech. It is living with divine dexterity and nimbleness that enables us to continually perceive, respond to, and cocreate life in imaginative, dynamic, and engaging new ways.

Prayer

God, may I know anew the lightness of heart I was born with. Amen.

A Non-Traveling Vacation

Have you ever gone on vacation to a faraway place and returned feeling more fatigued than when you left? Truly invigorating vacations are more about changing what's inside of us than they are about changing what's around us. In order to feel genuine renewal, a change of setting may help, but it's not necessary.

Here are four ways to have a soulfully satisfying vacation without booking a trip anywhere. How long you stay—five minutes, five days, or five weeks—is up to you:

1. Let Go. Release all activities that regularly absorb energy from you, especially all work-related actions and thoughts. Genuine vacations can't happen unless you vacate your mind of thoughts that can easily and often unconsciously lure you back into work mode. A rubber band on the wrist can help you avoid thinking about work. Whenever work thoughts surface, give yourself a little pop.

2. Lose the Schedule. Much of our daily anxiety is connected to our having to do this or be there at a certain time. True vacations take all the demand out of time. While on vacation, forget about having to do anything on time; live free and easy in time.

3. Delight Yourself. Engage fun, healthy, and wholesome activities for joy's sake. Submerge yourself in a spirit of play.

4. Love the Margin. Margin is the space between our load and our limits. Such space is virtually nonexistent in our "crazy busy" world. Savor the empty spaces in your vacation, the times when you are sitting, being still, and doing nothing. Aaahhh.

Whether or not you have made plans to get away physically this month, plan to get away mentally and emotionally. Your soul, your family and friends, and your work will thank you.

15

{ PEACE }

Take a Breath

The Hebrew word for "breath," *ruach*, also means "wind" and "spirit." To go through life doing as much as we can, as fast as we can, puts us at risk for breathless living.

Practice

Breathe deeply.

Relax your body.

Empty your mind.

Accept your divine acceptance.

Take your soul to a peaceful place.

Have some grace.

Observe Sacred Stops

That's enough! Now know that I am God!

—Psalm 46:10

In a 2003 *Jazz Times* interview, noted bassist Miroslav Vitouš spoke about his "new attitude about the bass": "This is where the bass doesn't play all the time. It's again breaking the traditional role of the bass, basically to set everybody free. When the bass stops playing, all of a sudden everybody's much more free because you have an equal thing going among the great musicians, and there's no one playing roles anymore. . . . Everybody becomes more free. It's a very liberating process" (Bill Milkowski, "Miroslav Vitous: Still Searching," *Jazz Times*, December 2003, http://jazztimes.com/articles/19683-miroslav -vitous-still-searching).

Plan more work pauses and stops this week. Notice what this does for you and those around you. Notice what it does for your dialogue with God.

Prayer

Lord, society applauds busyness, not stillness.
Remind me of your sacred preference for
silence and stillness. Help me know that there
are things about myself, life, and you that can
only be heard in sounds just above a whisper.

Action

Listen to Miroslav Vitouš's composition "Sun Flower" on the album *Universal Syncopations*.

Peace Pockets

Peace pockets are five- to fifteen-minute intentional intervals throughout the day for spiritual, mental, and physical respite and renewal. During your peace-pocket time, you may listen to soft music, watch a burning candle, pay attention to your breathing, allow your mind to wander free, or give it the freedom not to wander anywhere or think of anything at all. The goal is to be "off" for a moment. The more experience you build, the better you will become at observing your peace pockets. Here are four things to remember as you create your unique and soulfully refreshing peace pockets:

1. *Permission.* If you don't value your calm, no one else will. You have to become convinced of the meaning and value for peace in your own life. You have to become persuaded that you are a better person with peace than without peace. Convince yourself that stillness leads to peace, peace leads to clarity, and clarity leads to creativity. Should you begin to feel guilty and selfish about making more time for nothing, dare to believe that the deeper selfishness is not giving yourself such time. As long as you remain "crazy busy," you ensure that the world, including those nearest and dearest to you, will never behold you at your finest. That would be selfish.

2. *Planning.* Schedule daily and weekly times of stillness and be open to the unscheduled graces of free time to simply be. Planning them with the same intent that you plan your work signals to your consciousness and, just as importantly, your unconscious mind that claim-

ing your inner calm is as important to you as anything else in your life. As you place these pockets in your calendar, be sure you give them the same level of priority that you give to your most important meetings.

3. *Practice.* Don't just plan your minirespite; live it. Real change involves more than knowing you need to change, wanting to, and planning to. As valuable as that is, authentic change transcends awareness and desire. Real change is actually choosing to be different, to live differently. And sustaining true change involves trusting your transformation beyond all fear and suffering. It will help for you to partner with a friend to serve as peace support person for the other. Agree with each other to share how you have been intentionally exploring and practicing inner peace. You may want to schedule a "biweekly peace summit" at a restaurant or park to compare notes and celebrate peaceful hearts.

4. *Personhood.* Know that having regular periods of stillness helps you to remember that you are infinitely more than what you do. You are God's "fabulous you" apart from any accomplishment or achievement. God cannot love you any more than God loves you right now, not because of anything you have done or will do. Sometimes coming home to you means savoring moments of having nothing to do. (Kirk Byron Jones, *Fulfilled: Living and Leading with Unusual Wisdom, Peace, and Joy* [Nashville: Abingdon Press, 2013], 18–19, used by permission)

19

{ GOD'S LIGHTNESS }

The Lightness of God

Come to me, all you who are struggling hard and carrying heavy loads, and I will give you rest. Put on my yoke, and learn from me. I'm gentle and humble. And you will find rest for yourselves. My yoke is easy to bear, and my burden is light.

—Matthew 11:28-30

I once daydreamed about God having a problem. In my daydream or imagination, God's problem was not the devil or sin. God had effectively addressed both those problems at Calvary. In my daydream, believe it or not, God's problem was religion. Through religion, many persons believed that God was distant. And religion often rendered God in exclusive terms, as being really accessible only to the truly holy. Finally, religion often made belief and faith feel heavy. Religion made God burdensome. In my daydream, religion's way of portraying God and the spiritual quest as burdensome seemed to bother God the most. When I asked why this was so, God's answered, "Because even if you understand that I am close and available to all, if your experience with me feels burdensome, I may as well be far off and attainable to only a few."

20

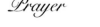

Prayer

Dear God, help me to feel your love, grace, and power
in a lighthearted sort of way. Amen.

Lightness, Light, and Enlightenment

Over the past several years, I have noticed myself interpreting spiritual truth in lighthearted ways. For example, just recently I have found myself hearing and writing the following thoughts:

Sometimes the soul just goes for what it needs. Pay attention to strange, yet uplifting impulses.

Souls were meant to soar; that's why freedom feels so good.

When we play, God is having fun through us.

Our being in love with life makes God laugh.

Let us engage this day with a lightness of heart that leaves the angels a little bit jealous

Such statements often just seem to land in my consciousness. In fact, their way of coming enchants me as much as the words themselves. I am finding that I am thrilled as much by the lightheartedness of God as I am by the light (glory) and enlightenment (wisdom) of God.

Journal about moments when you have experienced
God in more lighthearted ways.

A Wondrous and Easy Glory

I once received the following e-mail from my daughter Joya:

Hey Pop: I just got a great mental image while listening to this Gospel
tune on the train. There is one lyric that's repeated toward the end of
the song: "I bow before the King." After hearing it a few times, I saw
the King bow back.

This brief e-mail landed in my spirit with such graceful force. The
image of God's easy and ready affirmation of Joya and Joya's being sur-
prisingly taken aback by it filled me with awe and gratitude.

Prayer

Dear God, may my amazement of you be
surpassed only by my acceptance of you,
in all your wondrous and easy glory. Amen.

{ GRACE }

Come Out and Play

To feel
fully loved
by God
is to
stop hiding
and be
free enough
to come out
and play.

Prayer

God, help me own the ways I have developed
to shut myself in and away from life. Inspire in
me the courage I need to live freely and fully
with the life you have given me. Amen.

Who Do You Say You Are?

If you make persons feel that they are inferior, you do not have to compel them to accept an inferior status, for they will seek it for themselves. If you make people think that they are justly outcasts, you do not have to order them to the back door. They will go without being told; and if there is no back door, they, by their very nature, will demand one.

—Carter G. Woodson, *The Mis-Education of the Negro*

Carter G. Woodson's words evidence the fact that what we tell ourselves is more important than what others tell us. We have the power to nullify the faulty valuations of others about who we are by denying them and living free and full as God's beloved. Or, we can accept diminished definitions and insist on living below our calling. The choice is up to us. Who do you say you are?

Affirmation

I am God's child, loved from the inside out and the outside in by a God of lavish love and mercy.

Say Yes to Grace

My grace is enough for you.

—2 Corinthians 12:9

God never meant
for life
to feel
so heavy.

It is time now
to lighten
your heavy load, and
say yes to grace.

(Kirk Byron Jones, *Say Yes to Grace: How to Burn Bright without Burning Out* [Randolf, MA: Soaring Spirit Press On, 2011], epigraph)

Prayer

Dear God, yes to your grace. Amen.

Take Off the Golden Blindfold

Abundance is not just about material possessions, and prosperity is not just about money. Abundance and prosperity, more deeply and richly considered, are about vibrant health and vital relationships; our very souls overflowing with love, peace, and joy; and our minds and hearts being outlandishly blessed with lavish and limitless imagination and creativity. Material possessions, including money, are wonderful realities, yet to think of them as completely defining our understanding of wealth is to be blinded to the bountiful ways we are all more wealthy than we think, all the time.

Prayer

Dear God, thank you. Amen.

The Power of Cherishing

Genuine wealth is not about deep pockets; it's about deep cherishing. To cherish is to hold dear. What gives meaning and value to what you hold is the love with which you hold it. The wealth of cherishing is in the holding dear that consequentially embellishes our spirit, making us feel even more rich inside, no matter how small the object or subject of our cherishing.

Action

Reflect on the following statement: It is better to have little and cherish much than it is to have much and cherish little.

Own Your Inner Wealth

There is a story told of the musk deer of North India. In the springtime, the deer is haunted by the odor of musk. He runs wildly over hill and ravine with his nostrils dilating and his little body throbbing with desire, sure that around the next clump of trees or bush he will find musk, the object of his quest. Then at last he falls, exhausted, with his little head resting on his tiny hoofs, only to discover that the odor of musk is in his own hide.

What if the sweet sense of inner peace and well-being is not acquired but simply accepted? If so, therein is the ready and continual prospect of living *from* acceptance and not *for* acceptance. We can stop overreaching for something we always, already have.

27

Prayer

———— ✵ ————

God, grant that I am able to observe the wild
wealth I already have by just being your
beloved child. May this mighty awareness fill
me with untold confidence and propel me and
those I journey with to unknown heights of
common caring and uncommon creativity. Amen.

{ HOPEFULNESS }

Practice Holy Amnesia

Don't remember the prior things; / don't ponder ancient history.

—Isaiah 43:18

These words are particularly noteworthy when you consider that many of the verses before it have to do with remembering. Isaiah 43 is a stirring cadence of remembrance for a people facing the task of reconstruction. The beat is deliberate and steady on drum center until verse 18, when, for no apparent reason, Isaiah strikes a dissonant sound on the rim of the drum: "Don't remember."

A headline I read once gives meaning to Isaiah's strange stroke. The headline declared the following: "Dead Paid Off by Social Security." The article revealed that 31 million dollars had been paid to deceased beneficiaries who were listed as dead in the agency's own electronic files. I smiled and then I thought: There are ways in which the dead past can have too much influence over the living present.

Do not remember the former things when the past keeps you from actively and creatively engaging the future. Do not remember the former things when the past holds you back instead of urging you on.

Action

Identify two or three energy-sapping memories. Practice eliminating them from your mental skies, at least temporarily, until you feel your wings strengthening and your gaze burning brightly for the future.

The True Wine of Astonishment

This is the true wine of astonishment:
We are not over when we think we are.

—Alice Walker

Prayer

Dear God, thank you that I never know enough to be completely hopeless. Amen.

Hope

I once asked a woman
yet standing
after many blows
that have fallen many,
"What is it that keeps you, still standing?"

After a pregnant pause,
she responded
with just one word
pronounced as purely
as I have ever heard it:

Hope

Action

Identify those spaces and places in your life when the
only thing that kept you going was hope.
What do you hope for most of all now? What
inspires your hope most? How might you
inspire hope in those you live with and lead?

{ INSPIRATION }

Living Inspiration

I have a friend who has amyotrophic lateral sclerosis, commonly known as Lou Gehrig's disease. Diagnosed just a few years ago, this beloved wife and mother of two communicates through a device that scans the movement of her eyes.

Three sentences she wrote during one of our visits remain with me:

I feel blessed to be here one more day.

God has given me a peace that passes all understanding.

I have not let ALS define who I am.

When I first read what my friend had written, it was as if a bright light was suddenly shinning on my soul. My friend's testimony of blessing, peace, and inspired holy identity is still shining, and I hope it never ever goes out.

Prayer

Dear God, thank you for people who
inspire us beyond measure, and often just
when we need it the most. Amen.

Celebrating Our Common Fire

Great leaders freely trust God to inspire great vision in others, and to manifest that vision in ways that are sometimes beyond the leader's wildest dreams. Such leaders, rather than being consumed by "the illusion of sole divine ownership," are lifted and even tickled by God's moving in mysterious ways beyond themselves. Take for instance, the full wonder of the Resurrection: not only was Jesus raised from the dead, but so were his followers. They were and are raised from deadening limitation and fear to unprecedented heights of marvelous meaningful mission in the world. The Resurrected Spirit set fiercely and fancifully free that day—and each day since—is not just the Holy Spirit of one, but the Holy Spirit of many.

Perhaps the best inspiration a leader can give is to help persons become more aware of their inner flame and show by their living example that like the leader, they, too, can trust the fire that burns within. Brilliant leaders inspire others to discover their own brilliance. As truly inspiring leaders, leaders that see and fan the flame in others, we are called to allow God room to move in ways way past our being and our knowing. Rather than leading to a laxity and negligence about ministry, such widening of attitude and perception to include a vision of the fine and full flourishing of God's vision among God's people can create a dynamic new anticipation and excitement for ministry, transforming drudgery into thrill. (Jones, *Fulfilled*, 127, used by permission)

Affirmation

꒒ꕤꕥ꒱

I am as thankful for us as I am for me.

Dream with God

As well as being a book of history, teachings, and poetry, the Bible is a book of dreams: God's and humans'. Sometimes the dreams converge; at other times divine and human dreams conflict with each other. But the grace in it all is that no matter how distorted and diminishing some dreams of humankind, God keeps on dreaming. God's deliberate, creative, and relentless imagining of new possibilities is, in part, what makes the Good Book so good!

As God's dreams are remembered through daily devotional reading, we are inspired to live divine visions with deeper confidence and joy, and to risk dreaming new dreams of our own. The Dreamer-God never stops dreaming and breathing new life into creation. In this respect, devotional Bible reading for pastors, church leaders, and anyone so daring is a way of imagining or dreaming with God and receiving the fresh winds of God's Spirit.

Prayer

꒒ꕤꕥ꒱

Dear God, I dedicate myself to dreaming
with you, and daring to manifest our
best dreams in the best way. Amen.

34

{ RELATIONSHIPS }

The Resurrection of Community

Though that person be the Son of God, resurrection is about more than the raising of a single magnificent life. What Jesus, himself, did just after his resurrection from the dead suggests that resurrection is not just about him. What he did was spend time with a loved one in tears near an empty tomb, a ministry team in disarray in a locked room, and a couple of strangers in conversation traveling along a dusty road. As soon as he was restored, Jesus sought to resume a connection with those he had been separated from and to initiate a connection with people he was meeting for the first time. Resurrection is not just about the raising of a solitary life; resurrection is about the raising of life in community.

Action

Take a moment to remember some of the most significant forms of group life that you have been a part of. What made these expressions of community matter to you? What did you receive? What did you contribute? How might you enhance your current understanding and experience of life in community?

Family Matters

Former CNN anchor Bernard Shaw saved one of his most memorable newscasts for last. As the final moments of his stellar career were winding down, a colleague asked Shaw to share some final reflections with the viewers. Shaw's response caught more than a few persons by surprise. Shaw said calmly and clearly, "It wasn't worth it." Shaw then explained that the reason why his career wasn't worth it was because he had to spend so much time away from his family. Joe Robinson, author of *Work to Live*, secured further elaboration from Shaw: "Nothing conspires more against a loving family than work. After your kids are off to college, you will have spent more hours supporting them than being with them. They have the missed touches to show for it."

Each of us is responsible for cultivating a living balance that does not leave our loved ones out, a living balance that we can be proud of at the end of a day, and a career.

Practice

Designate frequent, preferably daily, family time.
Honor such time with the same attention and
purposefulness that you honor your work.
When you are with your family in person or
necessarily via alternative forms of communication,
be with them fully, in mind and heart.

You Have to Love to Lead

I once asked the late Cynthia Perry Ray, wife of the late Reverend Sandy F. Ray, what made her husband such a great preacher. She smiled and responded, "Sandy loved people." I nodded but felt that she had misheard my question. What she said sounded like a good answer to the question, "What made your husband such a great pastor?" I made small talk for a moment, and decided to launch my question again, "I know your husband was a great pastor, but what made him a great preacher?" She smiled again, even more broadly this time and said, "I told you, my husband loved people." I have never forgotten that exchange. What she said in substance was that her husband's effectiveness in the pulpit began in his heart. (From Kirk Byron Jones, *The Jazz of Preaching: How to Preach with Great Freedom and Joy*, [Nashville: Abingdon Press, 2004], 19, used by permission)

Prayer

God, inspire me to remember that all the strategies in the world cannot make up for a lack of genuine compassion and interest. Help me genuinely care about those who I work with and lead. Amen.

{ BOUNTY }

Don't Let the Low Places Fool You

Believing that God is everywhere invites us to be open to dynamic creative potential anywhere, including the valley of disappointment and discouragement. Remaining fixed on this hopeful perspective is essential to our not letting low places and feelings define and overwhelm us. Don't let the low places fool you. Some of God's best blessings are found in the spaces of our dismay. Stay honest, alert, expectant, and grateful, and deliverance will come, often in unpredictable and unusually satisfying ways.

Affirmation

I will look for lessons in the valley and
live like never before.

Warm Up to God's Generosity

While we grow up being taught to ask for God's blessings, receiving God's blessings may take some getting used to. Learning to receive God's blessings is one of the sweet challenges of life. Equal to God's vastness is God's lavish desire to bless. The ridiculously diverse bounty of nature is but one example. Can you warm up to God's generosity? How much can you stand to be blessed?

Practice

Notice the ways you are blessed today, from the smallest to the largest. You may want to even keep a list you may refer to time and time again to remind yourself of how wonderfully generous God is.

Embrace Overflow

"My cup runs over" is how David refers to God blessing him with blessing on top of blessing. Perhaps it's because he is a king that David does not second-guess being treated lavishly. In this scripture, there is no indication of him being uneasy with God's free and easy grace manifested in so many different ways. David is at home with God's gracious overflow. And may we be as well. There ought be no guilt or shame in being treated like the wondrous creation you are. Wonder is deserving of wonderful.

Prayer

Dear God, may I openly and willingly receive of your bounty no matter how glad it makes me feel. Amen.

{ FREEDOM }

Be a Freedom Coach

Once while taking an early morning walk in Philadelphia, I came across a striking sculpture by Zenos Frudakas. In front is a person in open stride, arms outstretched, face raised toward the sky. Behind this person are four vertical tombs. One is empty—the freed soul has just emerged. In the others, three more beings are coming out.

Instantly, I marveled, "What a picture of freedom!" Then I saw the writing in the empty tomb where a head once rested: "Stand here." The artist didn't stop at expressing freedom; he wanted viewers to experience it. I walked into the empty space and stood still. Then I took a delightful step into freedom.

Practice

Develop incentives and activities that encourage
those you lead to embrace and practice their
living and creative freedom without fear of
judgment or repercussion.

Live to Soar

While walking in my neighborhood one morning, I heard rustling in trees to my left. Suddenly, as I turned to look, a small red bird jetted across my path headed toward the other side of the street. A situation in which a collision is narrowly avoided is called a near miss. Perhaps this incident would qualify as such; when the bird crossed my path it could not have been more than fifteen yards away. On the other hand, this close encounter was anything but a near miss. You see, as the bird passed before me it dropped this question on me: *Do you think birds ever think, for a moment, that they shouldn't fly?*

We miss out on so much adventure and assent because of hesitancy and fear. We cage ourselves in jail cells of low aspirations. We resist dreaming beyond our comfort zones. We end up accepting stale acceptableness as our living norm. We don't fly because we don't think we can or should.

Practice

Reflect on the following passage in
Ralph Ellison's short story *Flying Home*:
"If God let you sprout wings you ought to
have sense enough not to let nobody make
you wear something that gits in the way of flyin."

The Nouwen Dilemma

Over the years, I have built up a certain reputation. People think of me as a Catholic priest, a spiritual writer, a member of a community with mentally handicapped people, a lover of God, and a lover of people. It is wonderful to have such a reputation. But lately I find I get caught in it and I experience it as restricting. Without wanting to, I feel a certain pressure within me to keep living up to that reputation and to do, say, and write things that fit the expectations of the Catholic Church, L'Arche, my family, my friends, my readers. I'm caught because I'm feeling that there is some kind of an agenda that I must follow in order to be faithful.

But since I am in my sixties, new thoughts, feelings, emotions, and passions have arisen within me that are not at all in line with my previous thoughts, feelings, emotions, and passions. So I find myself asking, "What is my responsibility to the world around me, and what is my responsibility to myself? What does it mean to be faithful to my vocation? Does it require that I be consistent with my earlier way of living or thinking, or does it ask for the courage to move in new directions even when doing so may be disappointing for some people?" . . .

Many new questions and concerns emerge at my present age that weren't there in the past. They refer to all the levels of life: community, prayer, friendship, intimacy, work, church, God, life, and death. How can I be free enough and let the questions emerge without fearing the consequences? I know I am not yet completely free because the fear is still there. (Henri Nouwen, *Sabbatical Journey* [New York: Crossroad, 1998], 168)

Action

Journal about the matters raised in Nouwen's wrestling of a confession. In what specific ways are do you share Henri Nouwen's dilemma?

{ CONSCIOUSNESS }

Plan to Improvise

Saxophonist Sonny Rollins is known for his expansive improvisational solos. He has been referred to as a "spontaneous orchestrate." Here's how he describes his experience with improvisation: "Whenever I try to create solos when I'm playing, what I am basically trying to do is blot out my mind as much as possible. Of course, I have already learned the material. After learning the material I try to blot out my mind and let it flow by itself. So I try not to really think too much about what I am playing when I am playing. I sort of have the structure already and then I try to create and let it come by itself."

One of the ways we attempt to manage countless chores and endless expectations is to plan our day out from start to finish, dotting every *i* and crossing every *t*. While planning and holding fast to a tight schedule can lead to significant accomplishments, it can also cause us to miss the gifted flow of the day, the ways in which life comes to us by itself. Plan your day with the alternative rhythms and surprises of life in mind. Plan to improvise on a moment's notice.

Practice

Leave grace spaces in your schedule, places where you are especially attentive to the unplanned and the unrehearsed. Note the quality of life in these spaces so that you can begin to welcome and trust them more.

Listen with Your Eyes

William Claxton makes the following confession in *Jazz Seen*, his wonderful collection of jazz-related photographs: "I love the music. Always have. But I've always been fascinated by the way it's produced, as well, by the way it looks. By the body language and the movements of musicians as they play, by the way the light strikes their faces. . . . I guess you could say I listen with my eyes."

When it comes to seeing, most of us are on automatic pilot. We don't think about it; we just look wherever our attention leads us, and usually not for long. Claxton raises the possibility of an alternative way of seeing: seeing with concentration. We know what it means to listen more intently, even if we don't do it often enough. Seeing more intently may be completely new territory. If Claxton's book is any clue, this new land of "listening with eyes" is well worth exploring.

Action

While relaxing outside, look around you.
Focus on a sight for several minutes. When
you are done, reflect on all you were able to hear, and
what you might have missed hearing had you not been
listening with your eyes.

Being Is Blessing

Just to be is a blessing; just to live is holy.

—Abraham Heschel

Often and innocently, we associate *blessing* with select acquisition and *holiness* with special ritual. These are "penthouse definitions" that lock us into believing that blessing and holiness have to do with certain extraordinary, isolated experiences. The genius of Heschel is that he discerned goodness and "Godness" to be constantly nearby. Heschel and his kind do not have to go far to experience deep peace and joy. In fact, they do not have to go anywhere at all; present being is sufficient enough holy ground.

Jesus said, "God's kingdom is already among you" (Luke 17:21). It is a striking observation, especially when you consider that conditions and prerequisites are not given. There is always something amazingly wonderful inside of us that we have nothing on earth to do with being there. It is a gift, and another reason to fathom that merely being is a blessing and just living is holy.

47

Practice

In sporting events, teams call time-outs to stop the clock and give more focused attention to strategy. Consider something different: Call a few "time-ins" this week to cherish the thrill of being in the moment, and the something thrilling inside of you.

JOY

Good Morning, Child of God

While away on a speaking engagement, an amazing thing happen to me one morning. As I started to rouse from sleep, I heard an inner voice, "Good morning, child of God." Though not an audible voice, the pronouncement startled me with its clarity and directness. I remained in bed thinking about what I'd just heard. What did it mean? Where did it come from? How could it meet me so firmly and finely in my first waking moments? I kept replaying the strange, powerful greeting in my mind, each time owning a little bit more of the potent affirming message it carried.

Moments later, while preparing to shave, I stared at the face in the mirror longer than usual. Soon, I heard the greeting again, "Good morning, child of God." This time the voice was audible; the voice was my own. (Jones, *Say Yes to Grace*, 34)

Action

Listen out for and repeat to yourself the things you
hear a loving God telling you.

Living in Celebration of Life

The score was lopsided in the early going of the 2014 West Coast Conference Semifinal Championship men's basketball contest between St. Mary's and Gonzaga. St. Mary's just seemed to be flat. One of the television commentators said as much in a way that was memorable for me: "They're not playing as if they're celebrating the game." WOW! Who let the preacher into the arena? The commentator's interpretation of St. Mary's uninspired performance ignited questions in my mind: What does it mean to play like you're celebrating the game? How does one live in a way that celebrates life? Do I preach, pastor, teach, and write in a way that celebrates each of those magnificent callings? What are the challenges to living, working, and playing in a way that celebrates what we are doing? How can we manifest the spirit of celebration more often in our being and doing?

Here are some starter answers to the last question:

Be thankful for being alive.
Be grateful for vocational and recreational opportunities.
Savor the experience of engagement with fellow participants.
Stay alert for the learning in the involvement.
Remain receptive to how the activity will challenge and
    change you for the better.

By the way, though St. Mary's eventually came up short, how they finished the game was a whole lot better than how they started it.

Prayer

Dear God, What a wondrous gift you have
given in giving life! Help me honor such a
gift by choosing to receive and live it in the
spirit in which it was given. Amen.

Have a Lust for Life

She was one of one of the most alive persons I have ever met. She had a bright countenance; her conversation was animated; she laughed easily at jokes (most of which she told); her eyes radiated invigorating energy. What made her all the more impressive was that this dynamic soul was seated next to a walker she relied on for moving about, a consequence of heart surgery she had while in her eighties. When I commented on her vitality, she responded that one of the greatest compliments paid her was from a person who said she had "a lust for living." I laughed aloud and said, "Amen!"

Lust is commonly regarded as an unsavory word, having to do with improper sexual urges and desires. The original meaning of the word has nothing to do with sexual impropriety, simply delight and pleasure. When life is truly a delight to someone, in spite of trials and troubles, that person has a luster, a luminosity, a bright light for all to see and behold.

Practice

Be on the lookout this week for persons who seem to have a light about them. Reflect on their attributes and what it is that makes them shine. Speak with one person you've observed. Ask about their love of life. Finally, with your reflections and findings in mind, if not on paper, choose attitudes and behaviors that will increase your lust for life.

{ GROWTH }

Seeing Yourself Stronger

In October 1979, Dr. Charles Garfield had an amazing experience. While attending a medical symposium in Milan, Italy, he began talking with a group of scientists who had focused their research on training athletes for optimal performance. During their discussions, the scientists convinced Garfield that they could significantly increase his weight-lifting ability by teaching him a few mental techniques. Garfield, who benched-pressed about 300 pounds at the time, agreed to be a research subject. The scientists put Mr. Garfield through deep relaxation exercises and asked him to imagine lifting 20 percent more than his 300 pound maximum. After forty minutes of mental rehearsal, they asked him to make the lift. After an initial failure, Garfield benchpressed, what was, in fact, 365 pounds!

Practice

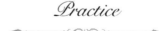

Take Romans 12:2 to heart and be transformed
continually by the renewing of your mind.

Remain in Learning Mode

I am learning all the time. The tombstone will be my diploma.

—Eartha Kitt

In chapter 3, verses 1-21 of John's Gospel, there is a record of a remarkable encounter between Jesus and a religious leader named Nicodemus. In this passage, we stand to learn as much from Nicodemus as we do from Jesus, although Jesus is doing most of the talking. Jesus is talking so much because Nicodemus keeps asking him questions: "How is it possible for an adult to be born? It's impossible to enter the mother's womb for a second time and be born, isn't it? . . . How are these things possible?" (vv. 4, 9). These are the questions we know about. Given the urgent matters being discussed and the intensity of the exchange, it is easy to believe that Nicodemus asked many more questions. This text is a picture of someone who, though accomplished, has opted to remain in learning mode.

Practice

Asking questions is a great way to stay in learning mode.
Ask away, every day!

53

On Not Settling for an
Earlier Version of Yourself

Introductory Biology, C

History of Civilization, C

Intermediate French, D

Language and Thinking, C

In all fairness, one of the reasons for Martin Luther King Jr.'s less-than-stellar early college grades was as that he entered Morehouse College at the age of fifteen. Because of the wartime draft, the school's enrollment was down and promising high school juniors were allowed to fill out the entering class. Even when placed into context, King's college grades are striking, given his historic achievements and contributions.

But that's the point—he did go on to make historic achievements and contributions, in large part because he kept learning and growing. In his sophomore year, King became a B student. During his junior year, he earned his first A. King went on to finish strong at Morehouse and to excel academically as an A student in two challenging graduate programs at Crozer Seminary and Boston University.

Referring to legendary jazz pianist composer and bandleader Duke Ellington, someone said that "he never settled for an earlier version of himself." King didn't either.

Practice

Regularly note specific ways in which you feel yourself becoming stronger. Continue to identify areas in which you wish to become stronger.

RISK

Peace in the Danger Zone of Change

Noted journalist Bill Moyers once asked the astonishing late poet Lucille Clifton about how she boldly addressed difficult, often heart-wrenching realities and themes in her poetry. Her immediate response was, "You cannot play for safety and make art."

There is perhaps a necessary inbred tension in religious experience. On the one hand, we are drawn to it, in part, due to the comfort and assurance it provides especially in times of stress and trial. On the other hand, the spiritual growth urged by most religious traditions, including Christianity, hinges on our being able to be vulnerable before change. Safety must be risked if transformation is to be realized.

Prayer

Dear God, where my need for safety is a blockade
to my being and doing better, grant me peace
in the danger zone of change. Amen.

Coming to Terms with Change

Church leader the Reverend Joan Brown Campbell once shared how she lost a good many friends when she, a white woman, publically aligned herself with the civil rights movement. Her perceptive observation was that her friends were not just troubled by the threat of physical danger due to their association with their friend, a civil rights advocate. Campbell felt something at work that was deeper than the threat of physical violence. She believed that her friends were even more troubled by seeing her change, and even more troubling than that was the haunting realization that if she could change, they could to.

Action

Take a moment to reflect on your feelings and thoughts about change. Identify the aspects of change that may trouble you the most. Remember your own experience with change as you seek to facilitate transformation in persons and organizations.

Practice Radical Openness

Elijah was used to God communicating with him through wondrous acts and miracles. In 1 Kings 17:6, he is fed by ravens. Later in the same chapter, a widow provides food for him, her last, and because she does, God keeps on providing for her. Next, the widow's son dies, but Elijah cries out to God and stretches himself out on the child three times, and "The LORD listened to Elijah's voice and gave the boy back his life" (1 Kings 17:22). Finally, in a showdown between the prophets of Baal and Elijah on Mount Carmel, God rains down fire at Elijah's call. Elijah was used to seeing God move in powerful, awe-inspiring ways.

This makes what happens in 1 Kings 19:11-13 (NKJV), all the more amazing:

> Then He said, "Go out, and stand on the mountain before the LORD." And behold, the LORD passed by, and a great and strong wind tore into the mountains and broke the rocks in pieces before the LORD, *but* the LORD *was* not in the wind; and after the wind an earthquake, *but* the LORD *was* not in the earthquake; and after the earthquake a fire, *but* the LORD *was* not in the fire; and after the fire a still small voice.
>
> So it was, when Elijah heard *it*, that he wrapped his face in his mantle and went out and stood in the entrance of the cave. Suddenly a voice *came* to him, and said, "What are you doing here, Elijah?"

On the mountain, God speaks to Elijah differently, yet Elijah is alert and open enough to hear God in a way he'd rarely, if ever, heard God before. Are you?

Prayer

Dear God, help me understand that the greater my openness, the greater my ability to receive your unexpected blessings in unsuspected ways. Amen.

SELF

The Sound of the Genuine

There is something in every one of you that waits and listens for the sound of the genuine in yourself. It is the only true guide you will ever have, and if you cannot hear it, you will all of your life spend your days on the ends of the strings that someone else pulls.

—Howard Thurman

Action

Journal with the following inquiry
and question in mind:
1. Recall instances when you definitely felt guided by the sound of the genuine in yourself.
2. Under what circumstances are you most likely to hear the sound of the genuine in yourself?

Sanctified Suspicions and Longings

There are still some notes that haven't been heard. I don't know where to find them, but I know they are there.

—Ornette Coleman, jazz saxophonist

Action

Reflect and doodle about things yet undiscovered but yearned for in your soul, relationships, work, and leisure.

Walking on Water

A voice whispered to me one morning,
"Come, let me show you
how to walk on water."

First, one step,
then another,
then a third, imagined.

"You see," said my teacher,
"It's not about what's under your feet;
it's about what's in your heart."

(Kirk Byron Jones, *Morning B.R.E.W. Journal*
[Minneapolis: Augsburg Fortress, 2005], 8)

Action

Think of a dream or aspiration that continues to tease
and taunt you. You may have given up on it, but it has
not given up on you. What small things can you do to
bring to life something that seems impossible?

{ Musicianship }

God Is a Drummer

The wonderful poet Hafiz includes the following lines in his poem "In a Manner I Won't Forget" as follows:

A father's toes lifting a child's in dance causes God to pull out a drum.

I used to play the drums, and I'm a big fan of jazz drumming, so the notion of God playing the drums is very appealing to me. Drumming is a way of catching and carrying the beat of music and the beat of life. Creative drumming not only captures the pace that already is; it sets the beat for what is yet to be. An invigorating and compelling beat can call forth new life.

Action

Journal (preferably while listening to "Watermelon Man" by Herbie Hancock or anything at all by the brilliant Jazz percussionist Terri Lynn Carrington) in response to the following questions:

How might envisioning God as a drummer transform your vision of God?
What parallels do you see between good drumming and good leadership?

Inspiring Others to Play
Their Song Their Way

The following words by Wynton Marsalis hold a wealth of knowledge for pastoral leaders and all leaders: "The most important thing you can do is to empower another person to be themselves—even if what they're going to do is going to be the opposite of what you do . . . you don't want to teach them dogma . . . you're a part of their story. A lot of times you [as a teacher] look at them as if they're a part of your story. You [should] try to empower them with tools to do what they want to do."

So often, pastoral ministry is presented in just the opposite light. I can remember beginning my own ministry with the intent to preach, teach, and lead people toward a model of Christian witness that I had come to own as authentic and true. Holding a vision of exemplary faith witness is an important attribute for leadership. Yet, Marsalis raises the possibility of overholding such a vision. Overholding the vision, no matter how applaudable the vision may be, makes us prone to missing the vision God inspires within others for mission and witness. Moreover, unconsciously subjugating the vision of others leads to ministry with a heavy hand, the goal being to implant our vision of faithfulness on others.

A viable alternative to ministry as imparting and impressing our way onto the way of others is to understand ministry first and foremost as inspiring others to play strong and true the unique song God has given them to play. Such a perspective immediately lightens the load of ministry. Suddenly, we are not obligated to change anyone or to persuade anyone. Our job is not to carry around an ideal understanding of God's kingdom or kindom (thank you, Ada María Isasi-Díaz), begging and pleading with others to carry their share of the load. Ministry is seen as something much lighter and more manageable, if not downright enjoyable. The goal is to point and inspire, not push and pull. The job is to help persons to see and sing their own songs, in their own words and notes. And while there may be some general themes that we hope will be present (God's faithfulness, love, joy, and peace), we are relieved from the duty of forcing people to express faithfulness according to the exact mandates of some dogma or creed. Substituted for the weighty demand of prodding people to conformity is the far more delightful duty of observing persons express their own unique faith witness in compelling and surprising ways. (Jones, *Fulfilled*, 128–29, used by permission)

Action

Note examples of unique characteristics
or presentations of those you lead that
inspire you and bring you joy.

Create Your Rhythm of Rest and Work

Though no two distinct musical compositions have the same exact sequence of notes, all compositions contain rests. Where there are no rests, there is no music. Similarly, though we all work in different manners and at different speeds, there is no sustained and productive labor without periods of rest. The challenge is to see such periods as significant as the work itself and to create our own unique rhythm that ensures labor never becomes devoid of rest. When that happens, the music stops.

Action

Create a workday schedule that includes two to four periods of ten- to twenty-minute respites and an hour lunch. Compare your experience of such a workday with days in which rest periods are not observed.

ENTHUSIASM

Riding Strong with Deliberate Enthusiasm

The following words conclude Lucille Clifton's poem "hag riding":

> and i lob my fierce thigh high
> over the rump of the day and honey
> (Lucille Clifton, "hag riding," in *Blessing the Boats*
> [Rochester, NY: BOA Editions, 2000], 119)

Some excitement for living seems to flow naturally: inspired by persons, experiences, and moments. Such enthusiasm overtakes us with little effort excited on our part. Yet, there is another kind of electric engaging of life that is prompted by our choice. This is deliberate enthusiasm that can be unleashed any time we desire.

Action

Living with deliberate enthusiasm is, in part,
a choice. How might you choose to do so
and choose to do so more often?

Undiminished Interest

If you asked ten jazz enthusiasts to identify the three greatest jazz
trumpeters in history, there is a strong chance that all ten will have
Miles Davis somewhere on their list. Dan Morgenstern identifies what
may have been the central key to Davis's ability to maintain his freshness of creativity as a musician and composer. He writes in *Living with
Jazz*: "Davis has found a number of tunes that are to his liking, and he
continues to discover new aspects and dimensions in them."

Having undiminished interest in anything is a choice. Davis heard
and found more because he chose and wanted to.

Prayer

God, Please pour your grace on the seeds of my sincere
interest and effort so that what comes forth will make
both you and me smile. Amen.

Don't Hold Back

Hearing cellist Yo-Yo Ma play is wondrous enough. Watching him play is to experience wonder on wonder. His entire body is engaged. He laughs; he sighs. He seems to be fully dedicated to what he's heard and played, is hearing and playing, and is about to hear and play. He is like a child—a God child!

Hearing and watching him brings to mind a story I once heard about another legendary full-playing cellist, Jacqueline du Pré. When she was six years old, having entered her first competition, she was running down the corridor carrying her cello above her head and bearing a huge grin. A custodian saw her, and mistaking her rapturous anticipation for relief said, "I see you've just had your chance to play!" Jacqueline answered, "No, no, I'm just about to."

In the beginning when God decided to create, God didn't hold back. Don't you hold back. Wholeheartedness leads to flourishing, and flourishing leads to fulfillment. All the letters for "success" are found in "sustained enthusiastic commitment."

Practice

View video presentations of Yo-Yo Ma and
Jacqueline du Pré. Give yourself fully to
what you love doing. Don't hold back.

{ REST }

In Praise of a Strange, Empty Day

A day where one has not pushed oneself to the limit seems a damaged damaging day, a sinful day. Not so! The most valuable thing we can do for the psyche, occasionally, is to let it rest, wander, live in the changing light of a room, not try to be or do anything whatsoever.

—May Sarton, *Journal of a Solitude*

Prayer

Dear God, let me not be duped by the lie that suggests holiness and busyness are one and the same. Grant me the trust to believe in emptiness and stillness. Amen.

Busy Does Not Mean Best

In his book *Crazy Busy: Overstretched, Overbooked, and about to Snap*, Dr. Edward Hallowell draws the following conclusion: "Being too busy is a persistent and pestering problem, one that is leading tens of millions of Americans to feel as if they were living in a swarm of gnats constantly taking bites out of their lives. All the screaming and swatting in the world does not make them go away" (Edward M. Hallowell, *Crazy Busy* [New York: Ballantine Books, 2007], 7). The great pastor and author Howard Thurman once said: "[Chronic] busyness is a substitute for the hard-won core of direction and commitment." In the words of that great Motown spiritual, "What Becomes of the Broken-Hearted," it is possible to be "always moving and going nowhere."

Practice

Review your "to-do" list and deliberately decide to focus more on offering up your best rather than just being busy. Work with patience, precision, power, and playfulness. You may not do as much, but your doing will be more meaningful and joyful.

Savor Scripture

I will never forget it. As I read Matthew 27:1-5, the scripture that chronicles Judas's fatal remorse over having betrayed Jesus, I suddenly found myself in an unscheduled moment of silence and meditation. I wondered about Judas and the depth of his pain. I wandered about the terrain of a different twist in the story: Judas turns Jesus over, but instead of allowing himself to be overcome by guilt to the point of suicide, Judas turns himself over to God's grace and mercy. Finally, I heard and listened to a voice in my spirit saying, "Tell them I was sorry." It was Judas talking, gently requesting that talk of him focus not just on his betrayal, but his being genuinely sorry afterwards.

My devotional reading called me to a place of wondering. To wonder is to allow the mind to loiter and to saunter about matters that call out to us to go deeper. Given the premium placed on moving fast in today's world, to simply walk about in body or mind may appear and feel like negligence. But, how else is mystery best served, but to engage it slowly and softly, as unhurriedly as possible? Such delicate engaging of scripture by pastors and leaders cultivates a more appropriate mindset and heart-set for receiving and imparting scripture. There is too much of that which matters most in Scripture to dash our way through it in mindless and heartless haste. The depth of God's word invites us to journey in faith and wonder, savoring as we go.

Action

Select a passage of scripture and read at your regular pace. Pause and read the same passage more slowly. What did you hear the second time around?

Saying Yes to a New Version of Yourself

I am about to do a new thing.

—Isaiah 43: 9

Edward Kennedy "Duke" Ellington has been called "the greatest of all jazz musicians" (Stanley Crouch, "Duke Ellington: Artist of the Century," *JazzTimes*, December 1999)." Among Ellington's most revered works are "Mood Indigo," "Sophisticated Lady," and the symphonic suites "Black, Brown, and Beige" and "Harlem." One of the highlights of Ellington's illustrious career was a series of sacred concerts about which he said, "I was able to say loudly and openly what I have been saying to myself on my knees" (Duke Ellington, *Music is My Mistress*, [New York: Da Capo Press, 1973] 261).

Perhaps the secret to Elllington's astounding creativity was his thirst for newness. Jazz critic Stanley Crouch writes, "Ellington was unable to settle for an earlier version of himself" (Crouch, "Duke Ellington: Artist of the Century"). Author Albert Murray reflected that Ellington was blessed with an "experimental disposition" (Ken Burns, *Jazz: A Film by Ken Burns*, episode 3 [Florentine Films, 2000]). Perhaps the best expression of Ellington's openness to newness comes from Ellington himself. When asked to identify his favorite composition, Ellington's answer was always the same, "My next one."

Prayer

Dear God, inspire me to hunger and thirst for
new adventures and explorations. Amen.

Leaping into the Unknown and Loving It

Cyrus Chestnut is one of the great jazz pianists of our time. Once before a performance he began by apologizing to all of us in the audience. Chestnut said something that went like this:

> If you have come to hear us play some of our songs that have become favorites of yours, I am sorry, you probably won't hear them. And if you do hear them, I promise you they will not sound exactly like you are used to hearing them. We believe that each musical presentation is different and should be. We expect a song to sound different each time we play it.

So taken with his bold assertion, I spoke with Chestnut about it after the performance. He explained to me that though he prepared and rehearsed regularly and rigorously, he felt as though each time he performed, he was leaping into the unknown and, moreover, that he was learning to love it. A year or so later, I took a leap and asked Chestnut to play/preach my pastoral installation service at First Baptist Church, Tewksbury, Massachusetts. Not only did he come and play with great freedom and joy, but he spoke to us about not only daring to get out of our boxes but also daring to risk standing on them and jumping, and while in midair saying, "Wheeeee!"

Such wild appreciation for the unfamiliar and the unknown, such an effusive passion to push the boundaries of who we are and what we do, has the power to revolutionize a leadership ethos too often gone and grown stale. Mind you, what I am referring to is not just a recurring fancy for the hottest leadership fad. I am talking about cultivating a newness disposition not rooted in keeping up with fads but grounded in an understanding that God is Creative Newness, and that such an attribute is in our sacred DNA. Creative newness is not something we have to fear on the one hand, or fabricate on the other hand. Creative newness is something we simply must own and celebrate with more deliberate and sustained intention—in the spirit and way of jazz musicians.

To do so would be to unleash an era of pastoral leadership not just able to survive in a crazy-busy world as manic as it is meaningless for many, but to thrive in such a world, offering compelling energy, guidance, and vision sufficient enough to inspire and keep on inspiring new life. (Jones, *Fulfilled*, 118–19, used by permission)

Affirmation

━━━━━━━━━ ⚜ ━━━━━━━━━

I own my innate creative nature with
sanctified pride and joy!

Catching Beautiful Breakthroughs as You Wake Up

Were you aware that you wake up on fertile ground each morning? The space between coming out of sleep and being fully awake is ripe. It is filled with dream messages that can enlighten. Additionally, one's own inner voice may be heard more clearly in a space not yet filled with the voices of others. Moreover, this is a time when the mind has not gone into hard think mode. It is still soft and open to matter we may too easily reject via our hard-nosed critical reflection. Finally, it is easier for us to hear God's voice when our own voice, as well as the voices of others, have not yet taken center stage. (Jones, *Fulfilled*, 72, used by permission)

Practice

Don't miss the blessings of early-morning soft consciousness. Place a notebook, recorder, or other device near your bed so that you may be ready to receive the gifts of first-waking awareness. Your simply showing such readiness to receive will have you receiving more. We often have not received because we expect not. Expect beautiful breakthroughs!

{ INTENTIONALITY }

The Gift of Choosing

Lazarus, come out!

—John 11:43

Though Jesus called Lazarus from the tomb, but he didn't force him out. Lazarus had to choose to come forth.

First, Lazarus might have ignored the voice of Jesus and pretended not to hear it. I remember reading somewhere that "the hardest thing to do in life is to awaken someone who is only pretending to be asleep."

Second, Lazarus could have heard his name called, come out, and then gone right back into the tomb. After all, he had been dead long enough to have gotten used to being lifeless. Sometimes we choose to cling to the familiar simply because it is familiar, no matter how deadly it may be.

Finally, Lazarus might not have exited the tomb at all, afraid of the changes that awaited him with the onset of new life. Newness is fine for most of us, as long as it doesn't challenge us to change too much.

By not fully owning our power to choose, we conveniently relinquish responsibility for our reality. This allows us to blame God and others for what happens or doesn't happen in life.

Choosing is a gift. Let us receive it and the grace that accompanies it.

Prayer

⸺⸺ ⟨○⟩ ⸺⸺

Dear God, thank you for granting us the blessing to
be cocreators with you by making choices. Amen.

Claiming Your New Life

Perhaps it was because it was Easter Sunday and newness was in
the air. Or maybe it was because of the full joy and confidence in the
preacher's melodic baritone horn of a voice. It might have just been
the fact that I was in the middle of a vocational transition and needed
a spiritual shove that would make risk feel less dangerous. Then again,
it is not out of the realm of grace for all three influences, and many
more beyond my understanding, to have been at work in that splendid
moment that has echoed in me for over a decade now. What struck me
and stuck with me since first hearing the late Reverend Peter Gomes
proclaim them that Easter morning are these words: *Christ has claimed
his new life. The question is, "Will you claim yours?"*

Identify five specific ways you wish to experience
something different in your life. Next, write
down at least two actions you will take
to claim your new dimension of living.

Prayer for New Life Making and Makers

Dear God,

Grant me alertness that I may be able to listen for and hear your Spirit, "the Voice of the Genuine," within me. Bless me with awareness that I may behold life with fresh eyes from moment to moment. Endow me with imagination that I may dare to envision different possibilities and choices. Fill me with deliberate creativeness that I may join you in transforming situations and circumstances for the best, over and over again.

Amen.

Carry One Day

Carry one day.
Put yesterday down.
Don't pick up tomorrow.
Carry one day.
(Jones, *Say Yes to Grace*, 78)

Prayer

Dear God, help me be more discerning about the ways
I tend to make my own load heavier than it needs to be.
I pledge to join you in the loving action of making
my load and the loads of others lighter. Amen.

Give It Your All

I recall hearing a story about a baseball player playing an extraordinary game the day following his father's death. Many were surprised that he would even play at all. When asked how he could play so well given the grief and pain surrounding his dad's death, the young ballplayer smiled and said, "Oh, you don't understand. You see, my father was blind. Today was the first time that he's ever seen me play."

Today has never seen you play; give it your all!

Affirmation

I insist on having an interesting and inspiring day!

Own Your Creative Power

All options are not considered until after you have considered creating new ones.

Prayer

Dear God, remind me of my inheritance as a
child of your limitless creative genius and power.
May I more fully embrace what is in me due
to your being in me.

{ ENCOURAGEMENT }

Never Counted Out

To the stranger in the railroad station in Daytona Beach who restored
my broken dream sixty-five years ago

The legendary spiritual pastor, teacher, and writer Howard Thurman might have dedicated his autobiography *With Head and Heart* to many great luminaries who first encountered him while they were still students, including Barbara Jordan, Alice Walker, and Martin Luther King Jr. It would have been a wonderful gesture to have dedicated his book to his beloved grandmother, "Grandma Nancy." Instead the book is dedicated to a complete stranger, without whom his sterling career would never have commenced. Young Thurman needed additional funds to cover the transport of his trunk to make the journey by train to attend high school. Thurman remembers:

I sat down on the steps of the railway station and cried my heart out. Presently I opened my eyes and saw before me a large pair of work shoes. My eyes crawled upward until I saw the man's face. He was a black man, dressed in overalls and a denim cap. As he looked down at me he rolled a cigarette and lit it. Then he said, "Boy, what in hell are you crying about?"

And I told him.

"If you're trying to get out of this damn town to get an education, the least I can do is to help you. Come with me," he said.

He took me around to the agent and asked, "How much does it take to send this boy's trunk to Jacksonville?"

Then he took out his rawhide money bag and counted the money out. When the agent handed him the receipt, he handed it to me. Then, without a word, he turned and disappeared down the railroad track. I never saw him again. (Howard Thurman, *With Head and Heart* [New York: Mariner Books, 1981], 24–25)

Because God and grace can never be counted out,
never count yourself or anyone else out.

Spotting God in Others

Once, while in a grocery store, I went up to a person I had not formally met to say "thank you." Though I didn't know his name, I recognized his face. It was the same full, jovial face I'd seen at a major intersection in our city for years as I drove our daughters to school. He was a street crossing guard who, while ably assisting youth and others across the busy streets, greeted as many drivers as he could with a smile and a wave. His smile and wave were compelling; they drew you to smile and wave back. It was sad to me, and I know to many others in the city, when suddenly he was no longer there at his post directing and protecting, and smiling and waving. So, when I recognized him in the store, I just had to approach him, introduce myself, shake his hand, smile, and say, with genuine gratitude, "thank you." Only God knows how many loads he lifted and hearts he encouraged with his grace-drenched smile and wave. And God would easily know because, in the fantastic mystery of it all, God was the one doing the smiling and the waving through him.

To believe that God may be found in anyone at any time may inspire us to live on the lookout for God, to be alert for God more often than not.

Practice

Expect to see something special in people. Be on the lookout for something in others that's unusually delightful and worth celebrating.

Even the Mighty Need Help

In his book *The Yellow Leaves*, Frederick Buechner remembers seeing President Franklin Roosevelt, who had been disabled by polio, in a hotel elevator:

> Even all these years later I can still remember the moment when the double doors of the elevator rumbled softly apart and there was Franklin D. Roosevelt framed in the wide opening. He was standing between two men, the taller of whom, my mother whispered, was one of his sons. Each of them had hold of him under one of his arms, and I could see that if they let him go, he would crumple to the ground. . . .
>
> What I learned for the first time from that glimpse I had of him in the elevator is that even the mightiest among us can't stand on our own. (Frederick Buechner, *The Yellow Leaves* [Louisville: Westminster John Knox, 2008], 19, 21)

Action

Take a moment to think of someone who can use some help. Plan to offer him or her support today, and do so. P.S. The person needing help the most may be you. Give yourself permission to seek and receive the help you need.

{ HUMANNESS }

Humanness and Spirituality Are Not Antonyms

In my youth, I was drawn to Jesus because of how amazingly divine he was. The first sermon I ever preached, at the age of twelve, was about the story of his walking on water. Interestingly, as the years have passed, I find myself being drawn to Jesus because of how thoroughly human he was. His careful attention to life and his compassionate way with people seem to inspire me daily. One lesson I learn from Jesus's brand of spirituality is that one does not become more spiritual by being less human. The wonderful preacher and writer Barbara Brown Taylor suggests that we consider that the highest calling of all is to be fully human.

Prayer

God, save me from the mistake of jumping over myself and others to get to you. Amen.

Coaching Creative Discomfort

Sometimes the contrary exertions inside us feel like gladiators tied together for a fight to the finish, and sometimes like the swimming bodies of yin and yang swirling around in the sane fishbowl. Either way, the opposing forces occupy a space that is like an ecotone, a transition zone between two ecological communities like forest and grassland or river and desert. They compete, yes; the word ecotone means a house divided, a system in transition. But they also can exchange, swapping juices, information, and resources. Ecotones have tremendous biological diversity and resilience.

—Gregg Levoy, *Finding and Following an Authentic Life*

Levoy's insight helps us engage transition more forthrightly. Rather than being merely uncomfortable in the tender places of change, we can be and coach others to be creatively uncomfortable.

Practice

Become adept at identifying and appreciating eco-tones in your life and organization.

Every Day Is a New Birth Day!

I once received an electronic birthday card via e-mail on July 2. It contained a marching band, a cheering crowd, and a skywriter all wishing me "Happy Birthday." I enjoyed the images and music but initially felt mildly resistant because July 2 is not my birthday. My birthday is June 10.

Yet, the more I thought about it, the more I began to free myself to accept the birthday greeting without any reservation whatsoever. I did so not just because of the thoughtful intention behind card, but because I realized that each day is a New Birth Day, if we so choose.

Each day, we may choose to engage the world afresh with new energy, desire, and possibility.

Practice

Cue a favorite song several mornings each week, and joyously celebrate your New Birth Day. But don't stop there. Intentionally cultivate your New Birth Day with inspired and creative new thoughts and actions.

{ TRUST }

Don't Be Scared!

Once, while shopping at a men's clothing store, I admired a nicely arranged coat, shirt, and tie combination. The salesperson wasted no time in assuring me that I would do well to purchase the arrangement. When I said that I had come into the store for something else, she insisted that I seriously consider the combination, casually suggesting, "It would really look nice with a pair of jeans."

"Jeans!" I screamed. "That sharp coat, shirt, and tie with a pair of jeans?"

"Oh yes," she exclaimed, adding, "Don't be scared!"

I had to laugh. "Don't be scared."

Well, though I have yet to act on the clerk's specific apparel recommendation, I have held on to her words. Being scared or afraid of this or that, over and over again, can drive the living right out of life. What is fear keeping you from? A dream? A desire? A relationship? New ideas? Yourself? God?

Don't be scared! If you can't resist, make sure you don't become your fears.

Prayer

Dear God, I bring my fears to you in trust
that they will not prevent my faithful
flight in this world. Amen.

An Unsung Remedy for Fear

Curiosity is an unsung remedy for fear. Try becoming insatiably
interested in what is scaring you to death.

Action

Write down a current fear and investigate it.

Trust Your Way Through

There is meaning in waiting.

There will be someone or something
to help you at the trying places on your path.

Unseen ground is not unsure ground.

Discouragement still has courage in it.

There are marvelous hidden lessons
in the valley moments.

Take strength from the struggle,
and trust your way through.

(Jones, *Morning B.R.E.W. Journal*, 34)

Prayer

Dear God, if I can't trust the way,
I will trust you, the Way-Maker. Amen.

{ AWE }

Stand to Be Amazed

My wife, our then-eight-year-old daughter, and a family friend stood there with me, four sets of eyes gazing up at a heavenly fireworks show. We were watching the Leonid meteors, dozens of bright meteors streaking through the southern sky. Actually, scientists say there were hundreds of meteors, only a few of which were visible to the naked eye. Given the brilliance of the few we saw, a full sighting would have been too much to take.

When I saw the first unusual launching of light from our porch I could hardly believe my eyes. It evoked wide-eyed delight, the kind that children are known to express on Christmas morning. I ran through the house waking everyone up. In the yard, we gleefully watched the meteor showers for the very first time. There were pauses between streaks, but that only made for more meteor excitement inside of us. As we watched with tiptoe expectancy, our imaginations began to take over:

The angels are playing catch with the stars.

God is snapping his fingers.

Heaven is having a party.

90

Action

Journal about the first and last times you were truly
amazed by something.

Behold the Small Glories

*Fragments of beauty and truth lie in every path; they need only the seeing
eye and the receptive spirit to become the stuff of authentic minor ecstasies.*

—Elizabeth Gray Vining, *World in Tune*

According to Elizabeth Gray Vining, minor ecstasies are "bits of
star dust which are for all of us. There's always a whole lot of glory
going on all the time. The flight of birds, the way the light lands on a
fence, the sound of children at play; glory never stops. Our job or play
is to be explorers of glory, especially the small glories right in front of
us every day.

Prayer

Dear God, may I become more aware of your surprising
and soulful expressions in the world. Amen.

You Can't Touch This!

Maybe it was the early morning darkness or the tears blurring her vision that caused Mary not to recognize one she would never ever forget. Yet, maybe there was another reason that Mary did not know him at first: Jesus didn't get up the same person he went down.

He is risen, but he is not the same. He is risen new. We know this is true, because of what he tells Mary when she goes to reach for him. MC Hammer stole the line and used it in a hit song a few years back. Jesus tells her in substance: "Don't grab me . . . you can't touch this!"

He is new, so new in fact, that in that moment, he is too much to grasp.

Well, the whole resurrection matter is almost too much to grasp. Maybe that's a good thing. Let us never fully grasp and get over it. Let there always be something about it that fills us with awe and wonder, and overwhelms us.

Prayer

Dear God, thank you for the wonder of it all.
May I not be fearful but rather revel in that
which is beyond my knowing. Amen.

{ COURAGE }

Taking Soul Stands

Early in her writing career, Alice Walker was asked by a leading national magazine to write about growing up in the South. Though Walker was pleased with what she produced, the magazine suggested major revisions. Walker refused. In a showdown meeting, Walker was informed that she didn't understand what was at stake here. She would have to change the piece or it would not be published. After considering the positive impact such an article would have on her budding career and weighing that against her integrity as a writer, Walker responded that they were the ones who did not understand. The only thing she had to do was choose those things that mattered in order to save her soul.

Prayer

Dear God, going along to get along is oh so desirable, and yet there are moments when I am compelled to resist. Help me be true to myself and to your Sprit in mine to know when to accept and when to reject. Help me take a stand for my soul. May such courage grow me and inspire others. Amen.

What Are You Willing to Risk It All For?

One of my former seminary students, John Reynolds, has written a marvelous book entitled *The Fight for Freedom: A Memoir of My Years in the Civil Rights Movement*. He includes an account of his first meeting with Martin Luther King Jr.:

> I do remember shaking Dr. King's hand and feeling totally in awe that I was actually meeting him. . . . Dr. King asked me two questions. The first was if I believed in, and could accept, the principle of non-violence. I remember saying that I didn't know anything about non-violence, but I was willing to accept it as a tactic. He said that non-violence was important to SCLC and it must be important to those who worked for SCLC. The other question was whether I was willing to die for what I believed in. (John Reynolds, *The Fight for Freedom* [Bloomington, IN: AuthorHouse, 2012], 36–37)

How dare Martin Luther King Jr.! What right did Martin Luther King Jr. have to ask of one who would follow him to be willing to risk it all?

Action

Make a list of things that you are willing to
give your life for. The list need not be long,
but should it be completely empty?

A Prayer for Organizational Courage

Oh God,

Fill us full to running over with the Courage of ANTICIPATION
not just for victories and successes,
but for process and dialogue;
not just for the expected results of sacred work,
but the unexpected rewards of the sacred work itself.

Fill us anew with Courage of CREATIVITY
that it may envision and dare
in ways never envisioned and dared before.

Help us to understand that
Sacred Creativity embraces Rest.
For Rest leads to Peace,
Peace leads to Clarity,
and Clarity leads to Enhanced Creativity.

Fill us afresh with the Courage of LIGHTHEARTEDNESS
so that serious and rigorous work is never estranged
from joy and laughter.

Without joy and laughter, our sensibilities are dulled
to the surprising ways you inspire and delight us all
all the time.

ANTICIPATION, CREATIVITY, and LIGHTHEARTEDNESS.
We own and trust our fresh filling with such things,
and offer our GRATITUDE ON GRATITUDE ON GRATITUDE
in response.

Amen.

GLADNESS

Vivacious Gladness

In her book *Long Life*, Mary Oliver reflects on what it is to manifest "a better, richer self": "I don't mean just mild goodness. I mean feistiness too, the fires of human energy stoked; I mean a gladness vivacious enough to disarrange the sorrows of the world into something better."

As I ponder Oliver's concept of "vivacious gladness," several questions start marching in my mind: What has the power to make me so happy? In what ways might I unknowingly restrain my wild joy? How do I tap into unchecked gladness more, and use that awesome energy as a resource for my creative work in the world?

Action

Ponder Oliver's notion of "vivacious gladness."
What questions march into your mind?

Get a Kick Out of Seeing
God Act Out in Others

The visitor was an internationally celebrated motivational speaker and corporate trainer. Meeting him recently and hearing his phenomenal story was a great thrill. I was deeply moved by his transformation from prisoner to respected empowerment personality and by his passion to touch the lives of others, especially our youth. To add to the charm of it all, our meeting was unscheduled; he just stopped by at the request of a beloved family member.

What if each of us is a unique expression of God, capable of bringing God joy in any moment? Can knowing that God gets a kick out of us inspire us to more readily get a kick out of each other? How much positive creative energy might be released for personal and organizational uplift by our consciously choosing to be more frequently lifted by each other?

Practice

Become more intentional about observing
and enjoying God's limitless dimensions
in other people, and in yourself.

Use Your Play Power

In the book *Fulfilled*, I discuss playfulness as an important attribute for inner fulfillment. Though play has repeatedly been identified as an integral part of unleashing our creativity from childhood through adulthood, some may still underestimate its priceless worth. If you are suspicious of play's value for human flourishing, take a moment to recall how you felt as a child playing with some of your favorite toys. Remember moments of raucous engagement with friends in your backyard or on a playground. Now ask yourself, "Is there a place for the energy of absorbing play in the person you are now and the work you do today?"

Prayer

Dear God, thank you for placing such a mighty impulse in us. We arrive here with a play instinct and disposition. May I never conspire with anyone or anything to douse the fire of such a mighty flame. Amen.

FEELING

The Gift of Crying

Let those who plant with tears reap the harvest with joyful shouts.

—Psalm 126:5

The girl's reading about her mother's fight against breast cancer started strong, but soon, overcome by tears, she stopped speaking. She stood alone at the podium with her big burden. Finally, she began again, and her story took a surprising turn. What many of us thought was the story of loss was actually a testimony of triumph. The girl's mother was still alive! Through pain and struggle, assisted by physicians and a loving family, the mother survived. The daughter's tears were not just tears remembering sadness, but tears celebrating gladness. (Jones, *Morning B.R.E.W. Journal*, 38)

Prayer

Dear God, thank you for the gift of crying,
for knowing that all the sadness and gladness inside must
have a way out. Amen.

Anything That Softens the Heart

Anything that softens the heart is of God.

Action

Write down ten things that soften your heart.

Best Grace

Sometimes,

so much

builds up

inside

of us

that crying

is the best grace

of all.

Action

Reflect on the place of tears in your life. When was the last time you cried? Have you felt the healing power of tears? Do you think there is a relationship between crying, cleansing, and creativity?

{ BREAKTHROUGHS }

Waking Up from the Familiar

John 5:1-9 (NKJV):

After this there was a feast of the Jews, and Jesus went up to Jerusalem. Now there is in Jerusalem by the Sheep *Gate* a pool, which is called in Hebrew, Bethesda, having five porches. In these lay a great multitude of sick people, blind, lame, paralyzed, waiting for the moving of the water. For an angel went down at a certain time into the pool and stirred up the water; then whoever stepped in first, after the stirring of the water, was made well of whatever disease he had. Now a certain man was there who had an infirmity thirty-eight years. When Jesus saw him lying there, and knew that he already had been *in that condition* a long time, He said to him, "Do you want to be made well?"

The sick man answered Him, "Sir, I have no man to put me into the pool when the water is stirred up; but while I am coming, another steps down before me."

Jesus said to him, "Rise, take up your bed and walk." And immediately the man was made well, took up his bed, and walked.

In John 5:1-9, before Jesus gets a man up, he has to wake him up. More precisely Jesus wakes the man from his fixation on what he is used to, what he has grown accustomed to. The question, "Do you want to be made well?" helps to lift something up and out of him. "I have no one to put me into the pool . . . someone else steps down ahead of me" (NRSV).

That was his familiar, what he had accepted as his living norm. If we listen real close, there is a hint of his having "mastered his suffering." In a provocative book about personal transformation called *Breaking the Habit of Being Yourself*, Dr. Joe Dispenza presents the following attitude of someone who resists engaging life fully and freely by choosing to stay with suffering:

> I've memorized this emotional state, and nothing in my environment—no person, no experience, no condition, no thing—is going to move me from my internal chemical state of suffering. It feels better to be in pain than to let go and be happy. I am enjoying my addiction for now, and all these things that you want to do might distract me from my emotional dependency. (135)

I don't know if such was the case of this man in the text, but whatever his outlook on life was, Jesus was getting him to look at it. Waking up from our familiar involves taking a look at the thoughts, ideas, and perceptions that regulate and guide us and cultivating a desire to imagine something different.

Prayer

Dear God, help me not to keep walking along the same narrow corridor of thoughts and ideas. Inspire me to explore the wider and broader range of living possibility. Amen.

Taking Up the Unfamilar

"Get up! Pick up your mat and walk," Jesus says in John 5:8. I can imagine the response being "What? You mean, I don't need to wait for an angel to trouble the water, and I don't need anyone to carry me to the water?" The man is healed not because Jesus wanted to heal, but because the person he wanted to heal was willing to have a dialogue with the unfamiliar, the end result being his decision to embark on a healing journey.

What if the man had said no? His breakthrough happens because he is willing to receive and act on change. His breakthrough happens because he is willing to break bread with a different reality. There is no breakthrough without our breaking bread with the unfamiliar.

Action

Take a moment to reflect on recurring new ideas and dreams you've had over the past months. What are some new "unfamiliars" calling out to you? What will your response be?

Breakthroughs and Breaking a Sweat

Breakthroughs are partnerships between divine initiative and human effort. If we are going to experience deliberate and dynamic development, we must be willing to break a sweat. And some other breakings may be involved, including breaking a bad habit or breaking an unhealthy relationship. Breakthroughs hinge on our sustained willingness to break out with new ways of thinking and being.

It's wonderful when organizations like the church can support us in our purposeful breakthrough being and doing. Yet, this is not always the case. Sometimes, organizations are more supporters of sameness than they are of newness. Therefore, be resolved to bear primary responsibility for breakthroughs yourself. Own your responsibility for your own renewal, over and over and over again.

Affirmation

I choose with all my heart, mind, body, and soul to go and grow in new ways, each and every day.

{ HOLY LUNACY }

Letting God Make Us Laugh

The story in Genesis 18 reveals that Sarah laughed to herself. It's a wonder she didn't break out in side-splitting, knee-slapping laughter. Who could blame her? What the stranger said was so silly and crazy that it was downright, well, funny. The stranger said that ninety-year-old Sarah married to one-hundred-year-old Abraham was going to have a baby. Sarah could hardly believe her ears. No wonder when she repeated it again in her mind she found herself laughing. Not that she wouldn't want to have a baby. In fact, she'd cried many times throughout the years, especially earlier on, about not giving birth. But a child now? She doesn't laugh to keep from crying, she just laughs and wonders if Abraham's dinner guest has had a little too much to drink. But as she begins to turn away from a conversation that she either accidentally hears, or has been eavesdropping on from behind the front curtain of the tent, she stops dead in her tracks. Somehow or another the stranger, the one who just made that crazy statement, is on to her; he has, somehow, heard her laughter, and is asking her husband, Abraham, about it. Amazingly, the stranger brings God into the picture. "Say it is impossible," suggests the stranger, "Is God not able to do the impossible?" Indeed, the text suggests that God is the one doing the talking.

Prayer

Dear God, thank you for making me laugh in
bafflement and in breakout joy. Amen.

Enemies of Delight

In the movie *Patch Adams*, a young unorthodox physician in training is almost dismissed from medical school, in part, for displaying "excessive happiness." In the movie *The Color Purple,* Sophia laments, "I know what it feels like to want to sing and have it beaten out of you."

In *Sacrifice and Delight,* Alan Jones indicts the church for trying to hold back laughter: In some ways the organization of the church looks as if it has arranged things precisely to see to it that the Spirit is kept in check, to see that nothing happens, least of all, the breaking out of delight.

It is possible to be so focused on order and tradition that we fail to appreciate God's great appetite for divine lunacy and sacred surprise.

Prayer

Dear God, may I ever be an easily recognizable friend of
delight and never its foe. Amen.

Discover the Clown in You

Dario Fo, one of Italy's great playwrights and clowns, won the 1997 Nobel Prize for Literature. When he was informed of this, he thought it was a big joke. Assured and reassured that it was not, Fo exclaimed, "God is a Clown! God is a Clown." We don't find those exact words in the scriptures, but we do find these words:

A joyful heart brightens one's face. (Proverbs 15:13)

A happy heart has a continual feast. (Proverbs 15:15)

Everlasting joy shall be upon their heads;
they shall obtain joy and gladness,
and sorrow and sighing shall flee away. (Isaiah 35:10 NRSV)

I will turn their mourning into laughter
and their sadness into joy;
I will comfort them. (Jeremiah 31:13)

I bring good news to you—wonderful, joyous news for all people. (Luke 2:10)

Happy are you who weep now, because you will laugh." (Luke 6:21)

Ask and you will receive so that your joy will be complete." (John 16:24)

He will wipe away every tear from their eyes. (Revelation 21:4)

Action

Doodle a picture of a clown. Imagine the clown being a part of God's Sprit within you. How does this make you feel? What new questions does it make you ask? What new ideas does it give rise to?

{ JAZZ IS ALL THAT! }

Jazz Is, Number One

Jazz is
choosing to
always remain
open to
playing
new choices.

Action

Listen to *Road Shows,* volume one, by Sonny Rollins.

Jazz Is, Number Two

Jazz is
living
radically
hospitable
to change.

Action

Attend a live jazz show. Pay attention to how
the artists pay attention and attend to creating
in the moment.

Jazz Is, Number Three

Jazz is the
rhythmic
exclamation point
to the Resurrection!

Purchase and enjoy the movie *Louis Armstrong: Good Evening Ev'rybody.* (How good is it? It features a performance by Armstrong and Mahalia Jackson.)

{ QUIET }

Getting to Quiet

Listen to yourself and in that quietude you might hear the voice of God.

—Maya Angelou's final tweet on Twitter (May 23, 2014)

Here are seven things that quiet me:

"Little" Jimmy Scott's singing. Jimmy Scott is a magnificent
 jazz singer who is still singing at his own unique, soulfully
 slow, sweet pace in his eighties.
A burning candle
Running water
Sunsets
Clear skies
Morning light in shaded trees
Rain

Action

Identify at least seven things that quiet your soul.

Lounging in God's Grace

God, help me to be still
to lounge
in Your grace
and listen
to Your song,
and to hear my song
in Yours.
(Jones, *Fulfilled*, 44, used by permission)

Action

Listen to the album *Alone* by Bill Evans.

Get Behind the Steel Plate

In her beautifully profound book *The Secret Life of Bees,* Sue Monk Kidd includes the following insightful passage:

> Every human being on the face of the earth has a steel plate in his head, but if you lie down now and then and get as still as you can, it will slide open like elevator doors, letting in all the secret thoughts that have been standing around so patiently, pushing the button for the ride to the top. The real troubles in life happen when those doors stay closed for too long. (Sue Monk Kidd, *The Secret Life of Bees* [New York: Penguin, 2002], 170)

Our steel plate can keep us from perceiving and owning our deep desires: what it is we truly want for ourselves. Understand that when you are still, your steel plate of ignorance and confusion is sliding open, allowing you access to the truths that will help you move on in your life with confident clarity.

Action

Draw/doddle/sketch a picture of your steel plate opening and some of the ideas and things that come floating out.

{ POETRY POWER }

Three Gifts of Poetry

In *When God Is Silent*, Barbara Brown Taylor says that Christianity is an "overly talkative religion" ([Boston: Cowley Publications, 1998], 74). She offers the following by way of remedy:

> In a time of famine typified by too many words with too much noise in them, we could use fewer words with more silence in them. This is a difficult concept to grasp, but you know it when you hear it. Some of the most effective language in the world leads you up to the brink of silence and leaves you there, with the soft surf of the unsayable lapping at your feet.

I smile on the outside and on the inside when I read Taylor's words. The final phrase of her quotation is her living giveaway as to the kind of language more than any other kind of language that may lead one to the brink of silence: "with the soft surf of the unsayable lapping at your feet." Such language is the language of poetry.

One of the greatest influences of all on my deepening appreciation for stillness, and the silence that may be had more readily there, is poetry. The fact that poetry's power in this regard is explainable doesn't render it any less amazing. First, I find that I have to slow down to read poetry effectively. To rush the reading of poetry is to risk missing its lavish wealth, which leads to the second power of poetry: its optimal use of the meanings and sounds of words. Because, poets use fewer of them, they don't waste words. On the contrary, they work wonders with them, evoking the deepest of meaning with just a few carefully selected and placed words—joined by pauses. And this for me is a third power of poetry: pauses. (Jones, *Fulfilled*, 21–22, used by permission)

Action

Read a few lines of poetry by a writer of your choosing. Note the power of the words and this exercise on you. How do you imagine reading more poetry can strengthen you as a person and leader?

The Poetry of Scripture

If you think my estimation of poetry to be excessive, hear the following words from Natasha Trethewey, current US Poet Laureate:

> Poetry makes us more observant, more compassionate, empathetic. [It] is our best means of communicating with each other, of touching not only the intellect but the heart. [It] is the best repository for our most humane, ethical and just feelings. We can be made to experience the world, interior lives of other human beings, by reading poetry. (Mary Loftus, "Her Calling," *Emory Magazine,* Autumn 2012, 25)

If Tretheway is even close to being correct, those who would lead ought to think twice before going forth verseless. Speaking of verses, come to think of it, some of my favorite Scriptures are prose gone poetry:

"The Lord is my shepherd, I shall not want. . . ."

"The Lord is my strength and my salvation. . . ."

"I waited patiently on the Lord, and he inclined unto me and heard my cry."

"They that wait on the Lord shall renew their strength. They shall mount up with wings as eagles. . . ."

"Ye must be born again."

"Ye are the light of the world and the salt of the earth."

"What shall separate us from the love of God. . . ."

"And God shall wipe away all tears."

The power of these texts is not just in their declaration; it's in their formulation—it's in the music! (Jones, *Fulfilled,* 25–26, used by permission)

Action

Read or recite several of your favorite passages
aloud. Be blessed by the message and the
music of the message.

Wait and See

I do not consider myself a poet, but sometimes a stream of words comes forth, like the following:

Sometimes
the best prayer of all
is to just sit in the sunlight,
and remember,
should it be temporarily
blocked from your view
that light hidden for a moment
is no less light,
just wait
and see.
(Jones, *Fulfilled*, 90, used by permission)

Action

Write a poem, or at least the first few lines of one.
Reflect on the words you have written. What inspired
them? How does the poem inspire you?

SPIRITUAL ENCHANTMENT

Angelic Whispers

A different angel
whispered
the same message
To each of us today:
Just be who you have it
in you to be
to God's Glory
and Laughter.

Action

Journal about the things about you that you
believe bring God joy. What about you makes
God laugh out loud?

Just Remembering

Should you ever
notice yourself
smiling
for no reason,
it could be
that your soul
is simply
remembering its Source.

Practice

Notice those times that a smile comes across your face
for no apparent reason, and just take a long moment
to savor your surprise joy.

A Cheerful Holy Spirit

A Cheerful Holy Spirit
is forever urging us to climb
over the fence of self-imposed limitation,
and roam free in the field of holy potential.

Prayer

Dear God, when I would walk away instead of climb,
keep urging, and where you can, lift me. Amen.

{ BLESS YOURSELF }

Honor Yourself

There are many marvelous pictures in *Seeing Jazz: Artists and Writers in Jazz.* One of my favorites was taken in 1941 by Milt Hinton. Hinton captured Cozy Cole, Danny Barker, and Chad Collins in a posture of greeting each other. In this perfectly proportioned, black-and-white picture (taken in my native New Orleans), the three men are tipping their hats and bowing to each other. It is a mundane, magical moment in which three African-American men in the pre-Civil Rights Movement deep South are offering to each other what a society poisoned by segregation denied them: respect. Just one look at the photograph and it is obvious that the subjects are doing more than welcoming each other; they are honoring each other. (Kirk Byron Jones, *Addicted to Hurry: Spiritual Strategies for Slowing Down* [Valley Forge, PA: Judson Press, 2003], 47)

Prayer

Dear God, you have gifted me and honored me with life.
May I honor such wondrous creation. Amen.

124

You Too

What if
at the
conclusion of
your singing
"How Great
Thou Art,"
You heard
God whisper,
"You Too"?

Action

Sing a chorus or two of "How Great Thou Art," and
then listen for God's whisper.

Be There for You

Being there
fully
for ourselves
allows us
to be there
fully
for others.

Practice

Each week, make and keep no fewer than seven ten-
to thirty-minute appointments with yourself. Do or
not do what you will. The only requirement is that
you somehow savor the solitude and yourself.

CURIOSITY

An Unsung Remedy

An unsung remedy
for fear
is curiosity.

Action

Identify a current fear. Begin an inquiry,
writing down all related questions that come to mind.
Notice the way merely asking questions draws you
closer to what you are exploring.

Still Praying

To ask God, "Why?" is still to pray.

Prayer

Dear God, why _____? Amen.

A Beautiful Question

A beautiful question is an ambitions yet actionable question that can shift the way we perceive or think about something—and that might serve as a catalyst to bring about change.

—Warren Burger, *A More Beautiful Question*

A belief that I have that grows in intensity each day is that questions are more important than answers. Whereas answers often shut down dialogue, questions keep the conversation going. The beauty of a question is its intent to know anew.

Prayer

Dear God, thank you for the fine edges, the places where new territory is perceptible and traversable through the beautiful archway of a question.

PRACTICING GRATITUDE

Practicing Defiant Gratitude

Beauty remains, even in misfortune. If you look for it, you discover more and more happiness and you regain your balance.

—Anne Frank, *The Diary of a Young Girl*

Anne Frank's words, and the testimonies of other courageous spirits who have faced this world's worst face, testify to the impossible-seeming possibility of defiant gratitude: the ability to savor sweetness while suffering.

It is necessary to regularly practice defiant gratitude in our delightful but dangerous world if we are to journey on in hope, and not be crushed to the earth by despair. One important key, it seems, to living this miracle is choosing. Defiant gratitude is not simply given to us, nor do we merely stumble upon it. No, this kind of gratitude, more than any other kind, is intentionally and defiantly grasped by the human spirit. Of course, the strength to grab is given by dogged God, who cries tenacious tears of grace and love amidst and against all hell has, or ever will have, to offer.

Remember a time when you or someone around you remained pleasantly optimistic in a trying time. Seek to exercise that same strength wherever and whenever you choose.

Deep Gratitude

Our gratitude may be rendered in an obligatory and hurried fashion. We mean no harm; indeed, thankfulness is meant and sent, but quickly. There is something to be said for offering gratitude slowly. In doing so, we take the time to more deeply savor that which we are grateful for, and to fill our gratitude with love. It may take a bit more time, intention, and effort, but the experience of deep gratitude makes what has been offered to us, and our offering of appreciation in return, all the more rich and enduring.

Do your best to ensure that persons can taste the thanks in your thankfulness.

Receiving Well

In John 12:1-8, Jesus is eating with his disciples and receiving the lavish anointing of Mary Magdalene. Judas, under the guise of missionary concern, attempts to end Mary's generous show of affection. Jesus will have none of it. He tells Judas, in essence, to shut up and mind his own business. The role reversal of Jesus as recipient as opposed to giver is significant, and so is the pictorial image. Not only does Jesus accept the role of the receiver, but he reclines into the role, savors it, and resists all attempts to snatch it from him. Jesus seems as used to receiving as he was to giving. I think there was a reason for this. The Gospels record times when Jesus removed himself from both the crowds and his disciples in order to be alone and receive something. That something, I believe, was Godly Acceptance straight from God. Having received love freely, Jesus was able to extend love freely in ways that incensed some and inspired others. (Kirk Byron Jones, *Morning B.R.E.W.: A Divine Power Drink for Your Soul* [Minneapolis: Augsburg Fortress, 2005], 59)

Prayer

Dear God, grant that I am able to receive your grace in order to share the same with others. Help me understand that I can't give what I don't have. Amen.

{ BEING GRACED }

Be Alert for Disguised Blessings

The story is told of a man who was shipwrecked on an island. After days of hoping in vain to be rescued, he decided to make the best of a bad situation and built a hut to live in. After searching for food one day he returned to his hut only to find it in flames, the smoke rolling upward. Bad had turned to worse. But, the next day something wonderful happened: He was rescued. He was beside himself with joy. In the midst of it all he asked one of the members of the rescue team, "How did you know I was here?" "Oh, that was easy," came the reply, "We saw your smoke signal!"

Prayer

Dear God, may I be ever alert to how
unique opportunities may come through
unusual adversity. Amen.

Amazing Grace

She spoke so gently and unassumingly that the gravity of what the church deacon said was softened but not missed. Earlier that day, it was discovered that her home contained traces of deadly carbon monoxide due to an obstructed chimney. Were it not for the cracks in the home, it was likely that she and her disabled husband would have perished. She smiled and said with quiet yet deliberate gratitude, "I am just blessed to be alive."

Amazing grace may be described as God meeting needs in us and for us that we can't name, and don't even know we have.

Practice

Take a moment today to reflect on and be grateful for your blessings, including the ones you can't name and don't even know about. Do so with no thought of your wasting time, as awareness and gratitude are two of life's most potent energizers.

Love Changes the Rules and the Game

I remember hearing a story about a youngster with Down syndrome who played Little League baseball. It had been a tough season in which he failed to even make contact with the ball when he was up at bat. He struck out each time. Toward the end of the season, his draught ended. He hit a ball that dribbled down the first base line. He was easily thrown out, but the moment was memorable for more reasons than one. The youngster not only made contact with the ball for the first time all season, but after being thrown out at first, he kept on running toward second base, and then on to third. Along the way, the crowd, home and visitors alike, got caught up in the player's elation. Everyone cheered loudly when he triumphantly crossed home plate.

Love not only changes the rules; love changes the whole game. Know yourself to be loved fully from within, and life will never again be the same. (Jones, *Say Yes to Grace*, 37–38)

Prayer

Dear God, may I know myself to be loved in such a way
that I see all rules and games in the light of love.

135

{ OPEN HOPE }

Practicing "Open Hope"

Tilden Edwards writes about the need to live with "open hope": "We never know just what the loving truth is until it is shown us as we go through the day from situation to situation. Therefore, our hope is not focused on particular expectations or results; it is more open and available to what we do not know and do not need to know until the time comes. . . . Such wide-eyed, open hope frees us to be more in touch with what is of God during the day, rather than being in touch with what we have predetermined by our too controlling and narrow expectations" (Tilden Edwards, "Living the Day from the Heart," in *The Weavings Reader: Living with God in the World*, edited by John S. Mogabgab [Nashville: Upper Room Books, 1993] 59).

Action

Journal about the notion of "open hope."
How do you reconcile it with the need for
planning and schedules?

Look with Fresh Eyes

Resist formulating your unknown future solely on the basis of your known past. Moment by moment, God's grace is birthing brand-new possibilities.

Prayer

Dear God, inspire me that I might match
the freshness of each new day with a
fresh outlook. Amen.

The Spaces between the Words

Could it be
that sometimes
God places the answer
to prayer
in the spaces between
the words of prayer?

Practice

Try speaking more slowly and using fewer words
in your prayers. Make sure that you listen as much
as you speak. Finally, get in the habit of having
a notebook, journal, or other device nearby.
Expect answers.

Divine Endowment

Claiming Your Divine Endowment

God's kingdom is already among you.

—Luke 17:21

"God's kingdom is already among you."

What does Jesus mean?

What is he saying?

What does he want us to think, believe, know?

Our merely asking such questions would make Jesus smile. You see, Jesus wasn't just trying to say something with this avalanche of an assertion, but he was trying to start something even more striking in its might and appeal: an enchanting and unending quest of our own into the sacred wealth of wisdom, peace, and joy that God has placed within each of us.

Action

How comfortable are you with fully claiming
(enjoying, exploring, and even expanding)
your divine endowment?

Watch Heaven Rejoice

Can you stand
living in light?

Can you imagine
sustained joy,
sharpened intuition,
and expanded intelligence?

Can you wield
the sword
of your own brilliance?

Answer yes.
And watch heaven rejoice.

Practice

Imagine yourself at your strongest. With God's blessing
and encouragement, live toward that vision.

Fanning Your Flame

In scripture, the image for inspired labor is flame. Moses is attracted to a new labor by a "burning bush." Jeremiah embraces a call to speak God's word by feeling God's word as "burning fire" shut up in his bones. The early church moves from fear to fearlessness in the wake of a great awakening characterized by "tongues of fire."

Our best offerings to the world are the things we are on fire about. When we are doing what we feel God's passion to do, God is glorified, we are fulfilled, and others are inspired. On the other hand, failing to perform our passion can cause recurring, seemingly unexplainable sadness, and, believe it or not, deep fatigue. Even more heavy and wearying than the fatigue of overwork is the tiredness resulting from our not doing what we deeply want to do.

Action

Journal responses to the following questions:
What do I deeply want to do?
What am I or could I be on fire about?

Divine Presence

We Are Never Alone

I remember my first car purchase and driving that new used car home in a rainstorm. My prayer was as follows: "God, please don't let me wreck my car." When you're in trouble, you don't pray long prayers. As I drove, from time to time, I would look in my rearview mirror. Each time I looked, I was encouraged to just keep driving and everything would be all right. The person I saw in my mirror was my father, Frederick Jesse Jones. He had driven me to pick up my new used car, and he was trailing me home. Just knowing he was there made the daunting drive doable.

Come what may, the reassuring presence of God Almighty makes the journey possible and more than worth the drive.

Prayer

Dear God, may I ever be reminded of
your continual presence in my life and the
lives of those I work with. Amen.

A Love Letter from God

Dear Child,

I love you for you. Let go, and let yourself feel loved. All the love you deserve and thought you never had is yours right now. But you must let me love you. All the sunshine in the world means nothing if you won't see the light or feel the warmth. Letting yourself feel my love changes everything. Let me love you, and then you live my love.

Love you madly, always have and always will,

God

(Jones, *Fulfilled*, 58–59, used by permission)

Action

Imagine receiving another "Letter from God." What does it say? How does it make you feel? How will it impact the way you live and lead others?

God's Being with You Does Not Depend on You Being with God

In the final chapter of the Gospel According to Matthew, Jesus promises to be with His disciples forever. He tells them this after having returned from the dead. According to the text, the risen Jesus is, in fact, speaking to a mixed crowd of believers and doubters. Why wouldn't there be doubters? A man came back from the dead, just like that! Perhaps the doubters feared, and not unjustifiably so, that the gathering on the mountain that evening was a setup to do away with as many followers of the dead Nazarene as could be done away with at one time.

Just a little less amazing to me now than the surprising arrival of the Resurrected One is the fact that Jesus does not divide the crowd before making the promise. You and I may have been tempted to separate the crowd into "believers" on one side and "doubters" on the other side. Perhaps we would have made the promise of continual spiritual companionship to the believers alone. But amazingly and graciously, Jesus does not split the group into two smaller groups, and the great big present of promise is offered to all present. Jesus doesn't need the doubters to be with him, for him to be with them. Similarly, God's being with us does not hinge on our being with God. (Jones, *Fulfilled*, 150, used by permission)

Affirmation

Even when I don't feel it to be so,
I trust that God is with me.

{ THE PRESENCE OF CHRIST }

What a Difference a Breath Makes

Then he breathed on them and said, "Receive the Holy Spirit."

—John 20:22

Marsha Norman's play *Third and Oak* includes a woman who has lost her husband. At one point she is in conversation with another woman in a Laundromat. At one point, the widow makes a memorable confession. She tells the other woman that, in her basement, she found a beach ball that she will not throw out because it is filled with her late husband's breath.

How much do you think the disciples cherished the breath of Jesus? How much do we?

Action

Picture yourself as one of the disciples being breathed
on by Jesus. How does it make you feel?

A Singing Jesus

Lord, dear Lord above, God almighty,
God of love, Please look down and see my people through.

—Duke Ellington

A former seminary student of mine is a gifted and imaginative
minister, musician, and composer. Once she shared a vision she'd experienced: "I had a vision: Christ's last words were not spoken, but sung,
and Duke Ellington was there. And 'Come Sunday' was the last song
of Christ. And Jesus sounded like Mahalia Jackson."

WOW!

Action

Listen to Mahalia Jackson singing "Come Sunday" on
the album *Black, Brown, and Beige* by Duke Ellington.

Letting the Fire Lean into You

Before I write, I light a candle. The flame keeps me company and inspires me. I say the flame. In fact, sometimes it's two flames: one candle with two wicks. Though a candle may have two wicks, I usually only light one. The second flame derives from my turning the lit wick toward the direction of the unlit one. Leaning the lit flame towards the other is what causes the unlit wick to catch fire. All the unlit flame has to do is be still.

The Bible uses fire in reference to ecstatic and very personal experiences with God. Perhaps the most famous flames are the burning bush on the back side of the desert that catches the attention and soul of Moses, the invigorating pulsating spiritual energy that burns in the prophet Jeremiah so it feels "just like fire" in his bones, and the tongues of sparks that take up residence just above the newly raised heads of renewed Jesus followers on the day of Pentecost. Spirituality in such moments is no static sort of thing; it is the energy of God so vibrant and full that it cannot contain itself within itself. It catches fire, enveloping everything in its path by fulfilling and thrilling scorching surprise.

Action

What if there is flame that is always leaning towards me and longing for me to catch fire? How does this knowledge change me?

{ THE PACE OF GRACE }

Live at the Pace of Grace

How Jesus came back to life matters almost as much as the fact that he did.

When Jesus came back to life, he took his time to lovingly greet Mary, casually walk with two persons who thought he was a stranger on the Emmaus Road, gracefully address Thomas's doubts, and gently encourage and reassure Peter. There is excitement in his return, but no hurry or strain. His resurrection is dripping with grace as much as it is with glorious new possibility.

The patient grace with which Jesus lived his transformation is a model for how we may live ours. In a culture characterized by doing as much as we can as fast as we can, to the point of stressing out ourselves and those around us, how soul-easing it is to know that personal transformation can have as much patience and grace in it as challenge. Change filled with grace is in the spirit of the words attributed to Jesus in Matthew 11:28-29: "Come to me, all you who are struggling hard and carrying heavy loads, and I will give you rest. Put on my yoke, and learn from me. I'm gentle and humble. And you will find rest for yourselves."

Paul reflects this notion of change at the pace of grace when he encourages us in Romans 6:4 not to sprint or strive in the newness of life, but to "walk in the newness of life." As we walk in the newness of life, we are more likely to stick to our transformation, to be less demanding and judgmental of ourselves and others, and to savor and enjoy the change process as much as the change result.

If we are willing, God is willing to transform us at the pace of grace.

Prayer

God, as I suspect leaves and flowers enjoy their budding before full bloom, inspire me to more fully notice, embrace, and enjoy your unrushed sacred grace change in me. Amen.

The Supremacy of Depth

The late George Duke, premiere musician and producer, explained how he came to prioritize depth of musical expression over dexterity, playing a lot of notes as nimbly as possible: "I got that from John Coltrane. As a kid, I snuck over to the Jazz Workshop in San Francisco. And some sax player was playing a lot of notes, man. I was astonished, but then 'Trane' came up to solo and played one note, and there was so much force and direction in that one note. I said, 'When I can do that, I'll know I've arrived'" (George Duke, *Jazziz*, November 2002, 15).

Speed has its moments, and sometimes those are crucial, life-saving moments. But whereas speed is salvation in some instances, it is damnation in others. One of the great hallmarks of Christian theology is eternal life, life after death. Rushing is a way of diminishing the depth of something else that should matter to us: life before death.

Action

Reflect on how you may put more into fewer things to gain a richer experience.

Take Your Time

I grew up in the African-American Baptist religious tradition in New Orleans. One of the historic and beloved features of my spiritual home is the talkback between congregation and minister during the preaching moment. Some liturgical-dialogical expressions are more common than others; one of the most familiar from pew to pulpit is "Take your time."

"Take your time" has multiple meanings depending upon the state of the sermon. A congregant seeking a deeper understanding may be urging the preacher to elaborate more, to furnish added information. Or, it is possible that the preacher is talking too fast and the expression "take your time" means "slow down."

There is a third possibility. Sometimes, preachers talk upon just the right words at just the right time. "Take your time" in this context means that what the preacher is saying is hitting home, is meeting a need. "Take your time" is a request for time to savor the portion given and a signal that a "second helping" (repeating a thought or phrase) would be appreciated.

There are unique moments, tasks, respites that should not be hurried. On the contrary, due to the special offering they hold for us, such experiences ought be slowed more intentionally and deliberately. (Jones, *Addicted to Hurry*, 107–8)

Practice

The next time you are moving towards the checkout line at a store, resist looking for the shortest line.

{ THE KINGDOM WITHIN }

Something Within

In his wonderful autobiography *Treat It Gentle*, legendary jazz clarinetist Sidney Bechet makes the following observation about the difference between bands that played just what they knew and bands that played what they knew and more: "You know, when you learn something, you can go just as far. When you've finished that, there's not much else you can do unless you know how to get hold of something inside you that isn't learned. It has to be there inside you without any need of learning. The band that played what it knew, it didn't have enough. In the end it would get confused; it was finished. And the people, they could tell" (Sidney Bechet, *Treat It Gentle* [Cambridge, MA: Da Capo, 2002], 68).

The phrase "get hold of something inside you" intrigues me. It reminds me of another something Jesus kept saying over and over again to people: "The kingdom of God is within you."

Action

What difference would it make if you perceived that spirituality was not so much about grasping for things that were outside you, but more about grabbing hold to things that were inside you?

What's in You Is Greater Than What's against You

You are from God, little children, and you have defeated these people because the one who is in you is greater than the one who is in the world.

—1 John 4:4

I remember reading a newspaper article about a local baseball player who had just been drafted by a major league team. The article was filled with accolades for this young pitcher:

"Going to be in the Big Leagues"

"A tremendous talent"

"His stuff is already there"

Yet the standout player had one glaring problem. At points during some games he seemed to lose all control, causing him to miss the plate by a wide margin. His coach was convinced that the problem was not a mechanical one, having to do with his delivery or the way he held the ball. Rather, the coach believed that he had a confidence problem: "He's always been good, but he's never thought he was all that good. Once he believes in all his talent, he'll be unbelievable."

Once we believe in what's in us, so will we!

Affirmation

Encouraged by the Holy Might within me,
I claim my sanctified confidence.

Journal Your Journey

I began journaling upon resigning my first full-time senior pastorate to pursue further graduate studies and a seminary teaching career. My main reason for writing almost every day in a small book filled with lined empty pages was that I didn't want to forget the wonderful persons I had loved, and the wondrous experiences we had shared during an amazing time of ministry together at the newly founded Beacon Light Baptist Church in New Orleans, Louisiana. I felt compelled to reflect on what I had learned and to draw applications from such reflection to help me better determine where I was heading. Little did I know that I would keep journaling long past this major transition and that my daily writing practice (which has gone through many different sized books of lined and unlined pages, and is now mainly being done via an iPad application called "Day One") would help me prayerfully and intentionally navigate many more life adventures, in both my outer and inner worlds.

One of the greatest benefits of journaling for me is that the practice is a consistently efficient and effective tool for genuine growth and transformation. Authentic change is not something to be passively desired, but something to be actively determined.

Journaling is a way to take responsibility for and practice deliberate, creative, and sustained personal transformation. By *deliberate*, I mean consciously and purposefully identifying specific areas in our lives where we wish to grow. By *creative*, I mean imagining and designing inspiring and practical strategies to cultivate our growth. By *sustained*, I mean mentally reviewing ways we have grown and are growing, and mentally previewing ways we wish to grow.

Life is a wondrous gift that none of us ever saw coming. Through the prayerful attention and intentional reflection of journaling, God's great gift becomes our great offering.

Action

Journal Writing Starter Questions:
1. What specific ways am I seeking to grow as a child of God?
2. What am I presently curious about?
3. What rocks am I currently searching under?

{ PEACE IN THE VALLEY }

Thank God for Thou

(Written the morning after the Boston Marathon Bombings, April 16, 2013)

Before we take on our earthly bodies, assume our earthly roles, and answer our earthly callings, we are the eternal beloved of God. Acknowledging this sacred limitless dimension of ourselves invites us to behold the presence and power of Divine Love in every predicament.

Sometimes this is so hard to do, especially when the innocent and blameless suffer and die over and over and over again. Yet, a broken heart may also be a tenacious heart. The root of this wondrous paradox is God's love, a love, mysterious and mighty, that is infinitely more relentless than evil is heartless.

David writes in Psalm 23:4, "Even when I walk through the darkest valley, / I fear no danger because you are with me." Thank God for Thou.

More than a few distressed and stricken valley wayfarers can join David in testifying to a truth that is just too good not to be true: No matter how deep the pain, God's love is deeper. Such a love, while not making us immune to the painful contradictions of life, might inspire us to agree with the healing awareness that spiritual teacher Howard Thurman affirmed in the aftermath of his wife's death. Thurman writes, "I was aware that God was not yet done with me, that I need never fear the darkness, nor delude myself that the contradictions of life are final."

As God's beloved, it is ours to behold love, through it all, and to journey on, with the blessed assurance that we are never, ever completely alone. Amen.

Prayer

Dear God, thank you for your relentless love. Amen.

The Blessing of Loss

It might be liberating to think of human life as informed by losses and disappearances as much as by gifted appearances, allowing a more present participation and witness to the difficulty of living. What is real can never be fully taken away; its essence always remains. . . . We learn, grow and become compassionate and generous as much through exile as homecoming; as much through loss as gain; as much through giving things away as in receiving what we believe to be our due. (David Whyte, "The Poetic Narrative of Our Times," *HuffPost* [blog], December 3, 2009, http://www.huffingtonpost.com/david-whyte/the-poetic-narrative-of-o_b_378536.html)

Action

Reflect on significant losses in your life.
Without minimizing the hurt, can you spot
the ways help has come through the hurt?

The Deepest Peace

While at a speaking engagement recently, we sang a song that I had not heard in a long time: "Jesus Walked This Lonesome Valley." Inspired by the traditional spiritual "Lonesome Valley," the song, in part, says:

> Jesus walked this lonesome valley
>
> . . . .
>
> He had to walk, walk it by Himself.

The song is about facing some of life's adversities alone, not because of selfishness on our part or heartlessness on the part of others, but because some challenges demand solitary struggle.

Certain hidden inner strengths reveal themselves when we have nowhere to run and no one to rely on. Yet, something else is true. Hidden strengths sprout amidst a hidden presence. Erma Moorman took the liberty to write a second stanza to the aforementioned song about God sending his Son to walk the lonesome valley with us.

Prayer

Dear God, may I sense your presence more and more in the valleys of life, and know the deepest peace in the deepest valley. Amen.

{ RECEIVING LOVE }

A Love Supreme

"God so loved the world that he gave his only Son"

—John 3:16

"A Love Supreme" is the title of one of the most beloved jazz offerings. Written and performed by the legendary saxophonist John Coltrane, the piece is Coltrane's interpretation of being awakened to God's boundless affection for creation and humanity. When you hear Coltrane play the composition, you can sense that he is playing out of the deepening and widening wells of his spiritual yearning. He genuinely desires to be close to God; he wants to touch God; he wants to be touched by God. Coltrane's longing is surpassed only by God's lavish response: a love supreme!

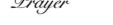

Prayer

Dear God, may I learn to accept my loving acceptance in you. In your love, I will rejoice and live free. How sweet it is to be loved by you!

Action

Listen to John Coltrane as bandleader and lead saxophone in "A Love Supreme" on the album *A Love Supreme*.

Take a Grace Ride

Living in Grace is
Letting yourself ride gleefully
Atop God's shoulders.
(Jones, *Say Yes to Grace*, 138)

Action

Imagine or doodle an image of yourself riding atop
God's shoulders. How does it make you feel to be free
with God in this way? How does this image of yourself
with God compare and contrast with other images you
have of yourself being with God?

To No Number

My friend tells this big/small story about her son. When he was much younger, he often shared his love for his mom in numerical terms. He would say to her, for example, "Mom, I love you a hundred million times." As he learned larger numbers, he expressed his affection for his mom in larger terms. One day, after his mother had done something especially nice for him, he launched into one of his loving numbers, but this time he became frustrated by not being able to think of a number he hadn't said before. Not wanting to admit defeat, he paused and said, "Oh, I love you to no number."

An adult now, "Love you to no number," is the way he signs all of his cards to his mother.

What if you knew that you were loved "to no number"? How would it make you feel? What creative energies does it unleash inside you?

Prayer

Thank you, God, for loving each of us, including me,
to no number. Amen.

SHARING LOVE

God's Grace Winks

A child skips,
A stranger smiles,
And God's Grace
Winks again.

Practice

God needs our help to keep winking in the world.
Do something small and slight to make
someone's load a little bit lighter.

Every "Good Morning"

Once, while walking in a park in Alexandria, Virginia, I came upon three women walking a couple of dogs. I stepped aside to allow them easier passage. As I moved back onto the path, one of the women smiled and said "Good Morning" so gently and sweetly that it startled me, in a delightful sort of way. Her "good morning" was more than mere acknowledgement of my presence; it was a genuine appreciation of my presence.

Practice

Try putting a little more love in
your "good mornings."

Fearless Abandon

May you
Be so
Comfortable
In Your Own Skin
That You
Are able
To celebrate others
With fearless abandon.

Action

Reflect on the words of the poem. How free are you when it comes to celebrating others? Are you as excited about the success of others as you are about your own success? Why? Why not?

{ STRENGTH }

Relentless Presence

God need not be named
to be known.
God need not be noticed
to be around.

Action

Meditate on those moments in your life when God just
didn't seem to be present. Identify whatever it was that
helped you make it through such spiritual nights.

Bless Your Boats

Lucille Clifton's treasure of a poem, "Blessing the Boats," trumpets the value of journey in life. Life is movement—with nourishing respite throughout—from place to place and moment to moment. Places aren't always geographical locations. Some of our most challenging trips involve transport from old ideas to new insights, and from entrenched allegiances to communities in tender formation. But onward we go, if we are to learn and grow.

Clifton invites us to love the journey "beyond the face of fear," and all the "boats" of people, ideas, and organizations and allow our "sail through this to that" (Jones, *Morning B.R.E.W. Journal*, 84).

Action

Reflect on the significant persons, ideas, and organizations in your life that have abetted some of your most significant transformations.

Benediction

Go in grace.
Step in peace.
Walk in love.
Just trust
that God
is with you,
and you
will always have
just the strength
you need.

Action

Keep having faith in a lighthearted sort of way.